BETWEEN HOPE AND HAVOC

Between Hope and Havoc

Essays into Human Learning and Education

Frank Smith

Heinemann • *Portsmouth, NH*

Heinemann
A division of Reed Elsevier Inc.
361 Hanover Street
Portsmouth, NH 03801–3912

Offices and agents throughout the world

Library of Congress Cataloging-in-Publication Data
Smith, Frank, 1928–
　　Between hope and havoc : essays into human learning and education
　/ Frank Smith.
　　　　p.　　cm.
　　Some essays previously appeared in various periodicals.
　　Includes bibliographical references and indexes.
　　ISBN 0-435-08857-2
　　1. Education—Aims and objectives. 2. Learning. 3. Reading,
Psychology of. I. Title
LB41.S63 1995
370'.1–dc 20　　　　　　　　　　　　　　　　　　　　　　　　95–34256
　　　　　　　　　　　　　　　　　　　　　　　　　　　　　　　　CIP

Editor: Scott Mahler
Production: Vicki Kasabian
Cover design: Jenny Jensen Greenleaf

Printed in the United States of America on acid-free paper
99　98　97　96　95　DA　1　2　3　4　5　6

Contents

Preface

The contents of the nine essays in this book range from hope for the almost unlimited potential of the human brain for learning and thinking, particularly through language and literacy, to despair at the individual and social damage caused by efforts to systematize teaching and learning in educational institutions. The essays were written over a period of a half dozen years, mainly in conjunction with workshops and seminars I was holding with groups of teachers. In consequence, the essays reflect issues especially important in our professional lives.

What the Brain Does Well focusses on that most personal and private source of individual power, the imagination, and *The Power of Language—First, Second, and Written* examines the way our personal identity is formed by the language we learn and the way we are taught. *What Happens When You Read?* relates the act of reading to every other kind of human experience.

Learning to Read: The Never-Ending Debate discusses why attitudes toward teaching reading and writing are sharply divided along ideological lines, and *Overselling Literacy* is concerned with how reading and writing are taught and talked about, frequently to the detriment of learners.

What Good Is a Teacher in the Information Age? looks at the role and influence of teachers as individuals, and *How Schools Must Change* extends the analysis to schools as communities. *Research: Getting on Top and Out from Under* considers how realistic are expectations that research will find the answers we seek.

There's a final rallying cry in *Let's Declare Education a Disaster (and Get On with Our Lives)*.

Earlier versions of five of the nine essays have been previously published. *Overselling Literacy*, *Learning to Read: The Never-Ending Debate* and *Let's Declare Education a Disaster* appeared in *Phi Delta Kappan* in January 1989, February 1992 and April 1995, respectively. The first two also had a limited publication, together with *What the Brain Does Well* and *How Schools Must Change*, through Abel Press, of Victoria, BC.

As with all my writing on education, I am indebted to teachers in many countries who have shared their insights, experience, and classrooms with me. One teacher, Mary-Theresa Smith, helped to shape every essay in this collection, and at the end she edited them all.

Chapter 1

What the Brain Does Well

There's a perverse concern in education today—amounting almost to an obsession—with things that the brain by its nature can't do very well. Commonplace things that the brain naturally accomplishes with unobtrusive efficiency are overlooked, and things that it finds awkward or difficult are emphasized. Thus life is made more complicated for students and teachers alike, and the brain has come to be regarded as a rather inadequate instrument for most educational purposes. It may even be "diagnosed" as defective, and prescribed special treatment.

I shall take a different perspective by concentrating on the positive. I shall discuss a number of things that the brain consistently does extraordinarily well, usually without receiving very much credit or even recognition.

My list of ways in which the brain excels consists of seven items. The first three are related to how we are able to interact effectively with a complex world just about every moment of every day. The next three concern important aspects of everyday thinking. Finally, there is an essential activity that the brain performs continuously and effortlessly, far better than any computer, generally overlooked by researchers and educators alike. This one superb characteristic of the brain may provide a better way to think about thinking than many of the ways in which human thought is currently studied.

Seven Outstanding Characteristics
of the Brain

1. Comprehending the World

The first outstanding characteristic could be called "making sense of the world"—when we proceed without confusion through our customary daily lives, organizing our personal affairs, doing a job, joining in conversations, enjoying books or movies, and engaging in all those activities which are a familiar part of our regular existence. There is no common term to cover all of this efficient "coping" that the brain accomplishes during the course of the day, though there are graphic ways of describing the condition when coping fails, such as "perplexity," "bewilderment," and "confusion." I refer to the positive state as *comprehension*.

We adults are all very good at comprehending our everyday world, despite its complexity, and so are children at comprehending theirs. Everyone's brain is packed with a voluminous accumulation of specialized "prior knowledge"—of faces and places, of objects and events, of procedures and relationships—that enable us to make sense of our own particular worlds. Psychologists call these elements of personal knowledge *schemas*, a bland term for the intricate distillation and blending of all the experience we have had in our lives. It is rare indeed, when we are doing something that we want to do, that we find ourselves confused, uncomprehending, and unable to make sense of the world. Comprehension comes easily to us in situations in which we are organizing and directing our own affairs. Nobody lacks "comprehension skills" who is able to get through most of the day without bewilderment.

The thread with which this continual spool of comprehension unwinds is *prediction*, which I would nominate as another superbly efficient characteristic of the brain except that I mention it later as part of a more general mental facility. We make sense of the world by anticipating what the world is likely to be like. This is an exquisite and subtle skill at which the human brain excels. Without prediction, there can be no comprehension; we understand what we anticipate. In other words, comprehension is a consequence of the inner control of events, with the brain directing thoughts and monitoring behavior along a coherent course of understanding.

The most common situations in which most people of any age are likely to find themselves with any serious lack of comprehension are "educational." These could be called *contrived* situations, when we are confronted by circumstances not directly connected to anything we already know. These situations are *decontextualized*—they have no location in anything that we can relate to, that we can turn to for support in comprehension. We put ourselves into contrived and decontextualized situations when we venture into areas where we have inadequate background knowledge and insufficient outside assistance. In schools, other people usually make the arrangements for us.

In circumstances that are unfamiliar to us, where we have little control over what is going on or insight into the motives of the people who brought the situation about, the brain finds comprehension difficult in the extreme. There can be no inner direction. Most of the time, however, the brain comprehends very well indeed. But this common aspect of efficient brain functioning has not been extensively studied by psychological or educational researchers, with the notable exception of Csikszentmihalyi (1990). Instead, comprehension is usually studied or tested in contrived and artificial circumstances, and as a consequence many individuals are frequently found lacking. Tests of "comprehension skills" may be deliberately constructed with a definite statistical likelihood that a proportion of students will fail.

2. Remembering

A second consistent and highly efficient characteristic of the brain is remembering—but again only in the course of the regular (but nonetheless complex) routine of our daily lives. We usually manage without effort to remember exactly what we need to remember when we need to remember it. We remember who we are, where we are, what day it is, what we are doing, and how to do what we are doing. If we need to buy something we remember what sort of a store to visit, where such a store is likely to be located, how to make a purchase, how to pay for it, and how to get home again afterward. All of this could be called "internally directed" remembering, as the brain gets on with its own business in the context of whatever it happens to be engaged in at the time.

Little of this everyday type of remembering involves stopping to think about what we are doing. We usually remember a little bit ahead of time, so that we know what we need to know when we need to know it. This is another aspect of the *prediction* which I have just said enables us to make sense of all the daily events in our lives. We remember just in time to anticipate what we will be doing or experiencing next, in an exquisitely orchestrated service routinely provided by the brain. No researcher has ever tried to catalog the innumerable things we remember on cue in the course of a day.

Memory lets us all down occasionally, especially if we are distracted. But usually it is only when we try deliberately to remember something out of context that it fails to pop into our mind. Memory fails, in other words, in contrived situations, when there is a deliberate effort to push it in a certain direction—particularly when that direction is determined by someone else. This is the test situation in school, when someone else contrives the circumstances in which the brain is expected to perform. And, as with comprehension, a child who fails to remember in such contrived situations may be diagnosed as having a critical deficiency which can only be remedied by specific instruction or "special education." This can transpire even though the child might be perfectly capable of remembering more relevant things on appropriate occasions.

It is not usually necessary to be able to remember "on demand" in the peremptory manner of many school activities. Such remembering is not the natural way the brain operates. Memory normally requires facilitation rather than training. If children can't remember what they are supposed to know, the cause is more likely to be that the demand is being made at an inappropriate time in an irrelevant manner than that they lack any critical memory skill.

3. Learning

As I have frequently asserted, the brain must be learning all the time; it is essentially a learning device. If we can remember what we had for dinner one particular evening last week, and where we ate, and what our friend was wearing at the time, then we must have learned those things. If we can remember the main items of the morning's news, and yesterday's sports scores, and last year's vacation, then these are also things that we have learned. The brain learns continually and consistently, without effort. It learns in the context of whatever meaningful activities it is engaged in, in the normal course of making sense of the world. What it learns is the basis of how it makes sense of the world, and how it remembers the appropriate things at the appropriate times.

If we are not learning, then we are bored. By definition, boredom is the condition we are in when there is nothing to learn, because we know it already, because we are not sufficiently interested, or because we are confused. All of these conditions are aversive, and we strive to avoid them. The natural state of the brain is to learn, which it does continually and efficiently as it goes about its own internally directed business.

How much the brain actually learns in the course of a day or a year is another matter that has been ignored in psychological and educational investigations. Subjects in experiments—and students in classrooms— are diagnosed as being deficient in essential learning skills if they fail to demonstrate rote memorization that has been arbitrarily contrived for them. They may learn a great variety of things about the experimenter (or the teacher), about the situation, and even about themselves, but if they can't reproduce precisely the specific facts or "data" that they are expected to learn, no matter how minimal their understanding or interest, then they are assumed to have learned nothing at all. And the blame is often laid on them rather than on the confusing situation in which they have been placed.

I have been discussing learning, remembering, and comprehending under separate headings, but they should not be considered separate "mental processes," distinct from each other or from the other aspects of mental life that I still have to consider. The brain is not partitioned like chapters of a textbook or periods in the school day. You can't have one mental function without the others. They are all part of the coherent and integrated manner in which we continually make sense of a complex and constantly changing world, in our own unique and individual ways. They are matters in which we are all enormously skilled. The reason this great mental power is frequently not exhibited in classrooms is that all too often the brain is expected to learn, remember, and comprehend at the instigation of someone else, in precisely the contrived, decontextualized, irrelevant, and sometimes threatening circumstances in which the brain does not function very well at all.

4. Reasoning

If reasoning is defined as drawing conclusions or making decisions, then the human brain must also be seen as reasoning all the time, and doing it well. Every perception we make is a conclusion that we draw—we *decide* that we are looking at a tree, hearing a particular song, smelling a rose, tasting peppermint, touching an oily surface. We *conclude* that it is safe to cross the road, time to have lunch, inappropriate to wear shorts, too soon to buy another pair of shoes, propitious to make a new friend. We would be reluctant to leave our homes in the morning if it were not for the confidence we have in our ability to make decisions swiftly, consistently, and well, whenever it is necessary for us to do so in the course of our daily affairs. We exercise this ability so effortlessly and effectively that we fail to recognize that we are doing so, and we rarely give ourselves and others credit for the ability. We don't usually make mistakes.

Of course, the ability fails us sometimes. We find ourselves reluctant or unable to make decisions, or we make decisions that we later regret or conclude were wrong. But inability to decide is usually a result of not having sufficient facts or of being apprehensive about consequences, rather than a lack of any essential skills.

At first glance my statement that everyone is naturally good at reasoning might be regarded as provocative, if not ridiculous. After all, reasoning is widely believed to be one of the basic "thinking skills" that children lack unless they are the recipients of specialized formal instruction. They are supposed to need training in *logical* reasoning skills. But this is all in a typical educational context of arbitrarily concocted fragments of exercises and tests. In the real world, everyone can think logically, and if they don't do so on occasion it is because they can do something more appropriate to the particular situation.

The problem with logic is its rigidity—and the fact that it can never be relied on to give a useful or dependable result. Logic never guarantees the right answer, or even a good one. All that logic can offer is a conclusion that is "valid," that follows inevitably from its premises. But it cannot tell if the premises are flawed or a conclusion is unsound. Logic can frequently lead to stupid and unacceptable decisions. This is the reason that computers programmed to follow inexorably any predetermined sequence of logical steps—and also logically minded administrators and bureaucrats—can come to absurd and occasionally dangerous conclusions. Individuals have qualities that bureaucracies and computers abysmally lack, namely feelings, values, and common sense.

In our normal thinking we do not tinker with the basic "rules" of logic, but we modify the premises or alter the conclusions when we think them inappropriate. We do this quite unconsciously. Given an argument based on assumptions which we do not share, we tend to misread or mishear the premises so that we can reason from the way in which we perceive the world. If logic leads to a conclusion that we find unacceptable, we reason our way to a more tolerable one.

The Russian psychologist Luria (1976) gives many examples of illiterate (but not ignorant) Russian peasants responding spontaneously to such formal syllogisms as *"In the Far North . . . all bears are white. Novaya Zemlya is in the Far North . . . What color are the bears there?"* The thoughtful replies include, *"I don't know, I've seen a black bear, I've never seen any others . . .";* *"There are different kinds of bears . . .";* *"I've never seen one, and hence I can't say . . .";* *"Your words can only be answered by someone who was there, and if a person wasn't there he can't say anything on the basis of your words."*

What interferes with formal reasoning, in other words, is *intelligence*. We reach conclusions that other people might dispute, not because we fail to exercise logic, but because we have different points of view. The persistence of so many religious, political, and scientific controversies, even among people of impeccable intellectual qualifications and manifest good will, is clear evidence that "logic" can't be the ruling principle underlying the decisions and conclusions we make about the world. We are governed by our values.

The ability of individuals to think (and to learn to exercise thought) depends not on the acquisition of special skills but on three other critical factors: prior knowledge, personal disposition, and authority. Reasoning is always "about something"—if we don't understand what we are supposed to be reasoning about, we can't reason effectively, no matter how skilled we might otherwise be. Good chess players or renowned detectives are not necessarily good writers, automobile mechanics, lawyers, or teachers. And no amount of generalized training in "thinking" will make anyone better at any of these activities. Individuals don't necessarily have the disposition or the authority to think in ways which lead to particularly challenging or upsetting conclusions, whether for themselves or for others. And it is not easy to reason in situations that are controlled by others. The "research evidence" that people can't reason very well is almost always based on contrived situations and contrived problems—on trivial puzzles, riddles, and tricks.

The brain reasons perfectly well because it has been reasoning from birth, all the time we are learning, remembering, and comprehending the world. Reasoning is an essential and central part of the way we make sense of the world—when our own brains are in charge and "problems" are not arbitrarily devised for us by others in the form of tests or educational obstacle courses. Our lives would be incoherent and chaotic if we were not constantly evaluating where we are now and how we plan to deal with the future. The very consistency of our view of ourselves and of our relationships with others around us reflects the powerful ways in which reasoning holds the world together for us.

How can I say that the brain at the same time does all these things I have so far discussed—the comprehending, remembering, learning, and reasoning? Because they are all part of the same continual ongoing process of making our way through the world. We remember in order to understand and to act in a rational way, and as we do this we learn. And the cement that holds everything together is my next topic—imagination.

5. Imagining

Our brains are rarely given credit for the amount and quality of the imagining they do, or for the necessity of doing it. Imagination is sometimes seen as an "escapist" activity, pointless daydreaming that is an idle alternative to the confrontation of reality.

It is true that much of our imagining has little to do with the immediate reality of our here and now. We engage in wishful thinking about the future or in rueful reflection about the past. But both are important aspects of how we are able to function effectively in the pressing world of the present. Wishful thinking can be rehearsal for the future, as we run through significant things we might say, enterprises we might undertake, gourmet meals we might cook—if only the opportunity were to arise. Invention of how we might have done something better in the past becomes preparation for the future. Imagination can stand in the stead of unattainable or undesirable realities.

But imagination is more than a way of leading a life separate from the events that daily envelop us. Imagination is the basis of our understanding and learning about the world in which we exist—it is the source of the *prediction* which I have already mentioned as the only way in which we can cope with the complexity and change in which our lives are embedded from moment to moment. What we cannot imagine, we cannot remember, understand, learn, or think about. Fantasy is not an idle manipulation of reality, but the construction of potential worlds. Reality is a fantasy that works, just one version of an infinite set of possibilities that the brain continually makes available to us.

Imagination generates alternative worlds, like a creative artist, and then selects among them on the basis of its own intentions or experience. We create the worlds we think most desirable or more likely, and then try to see if they work—if they "fit." Successful artists usually excel at one of these aspects of creativity, but not always both. T. S. Eliot produced many wonderful lines of poetry, but could not always select the most appropriate ones for a compact and compelling poem. Fortunately he had as an editor Ezra Pound, who as a critic did not have perhaps the same dramatic vision, but who could recognize the right lines when he saw them.

The human brain is a marvellous imagining device, especially in children, generating and selecting the most appropriate alternatives, not so much for "art" as for daily experience. Many psycholinguists have asserted that infants must *invent* language in order to learn to use it. Children must imagine what the relationships might be between the sounds and signs that people produce and the intentions behind them, and they need to imagine the underlying rules that make language systematic and productive. No instruction can tell these things to children.

Another way of looking at the continual imagining of the brain—at the continual generation of possible explanations of events and anticipations of how they might turn out—is that the brain is an avid storyteller and consumer of stories. It is essentially by generating and comprehending *narratives* that the brain makes sense of the world and operates upon it. The brain expects events to have a reason, a beginning, middle, and end, with characters, plots, motives, and appropriate relationships. As William James (1890), Rosen (1986), and Bruner (1986) all observed, the brain is a narrative device. The brain *knows* what stories are, even though it has to learn the particular conventions of stories that it hears related, or sees acted out. It naturally enjoys inventing them and sharing them. Narrative-telling and understanding are again effortlessly accomplished in the normal course of meaningful events in which we are involved. Imagination is no special faculty; it is just another aspect of living. Children imagine all the time, often blurring the edges of fantasy and reality. Adults are not immune to this.

Imagination is difficult only when it is contrived—when we try to force ourselves to think "creatively" about something that we are just not comfortable thinking about at all, or when someone else requires us to do so. And once again if you consult the research, especially in education, you will find that imagination has typically been studied in controlled, artificial situations, where the brain is constrained rather than liberated in its endeavors. Such artificial research can actually lead to suggestions that children lack imagination, or that they need to be taught creative thinking skills. But if children appear to be incapable of imagining, then there must be something wrong with the circumstances they are in. One of the few researchers into creative thinking who has given children due credit for their achievements is Perkins (1981). Imagining is not difficult or stressful; it is the normal mode of operation of the brain.

6. Insight and Intuition

A particular aspect of efficient mental activity at which human beings routinely excel is in the dramatic achievement of inferences or the solution of problems without conscious "reasoning" or sustained effort. Either the notion just pops into our head (insight) or we have a strong and pervasive feeling (intuition). While neither insight nor intuition has been studied or analyzed intensively—except to try to explain them away—no research has ever shown that the results of intuition and insight, however they are achieved, are not usually successful and reliable.

Insight is an imaginative mode of thinking, the brain quietly ticking over, generating and examining possibilities until an alternative comes up which "fits" as an explanation or solution for a particular situation or concern. Insight, in other words, is no different from the more general aspects of imaginative creativity—the generation of likely or useful alternatives and the selection of the most appropriate one.

Intuitive or insightful thinking is hardly likely to be demonstrated in contrived situations, under external control. But when the brain is free to attend to its own internal affairs, it is probably constantly engaged in intuitive and insightful activities. We have a feeling about a person or a problem, and we set about finding a justification for it, or for dismissing it. Intuitions generally arrive with great force, not, I think, because they are "subjective," with the blind power of emotional urging, but because they are *intellectual*, based on knowledge and derived from a painstaking reflection that is not accessible to consciousness.

To try to explain intuition and insight I must move on to the final aspect of everyday brain activity that remains to be discussed. This seventh characteristic is something at which the human brain is incredibly skilled, far better than any computer is ever likely to be, and may well be at the core of all the other aspects of naturally skilled brain function that I have listed. Yet this characteristic has been widely ignored by researchers, probably because we accomplish it so effortlessly. It is a universal talent almost completely taken for granted. Once again, there is not even a common word for it in our everyday language. I shall refer to it by the technical name of pattern recognition.

7. Pattern recognition

Pattern recognition is the term employed by research psychologists to refer to the ability to identify visible objects in the world around us, such as letters of the alphabet, or written words. In order to say what the letter *K* is, for example, we first have to recognize it; we must be able to distinguish the pattern of marks that constitute the letter *K* from the patterns of marks that make up other letters of the alphabet, and everything else that can be distinguished visually.

Despite the confusions which children occasionally encounter in learning the letters of the alphabet, human beings in general are superb pattern recognizers. The difficulty children occasionally experience with the alphabet usually has more to do with uncertainty or unfamiliarity in contrived situations than with problems in seeing. Everyone who can see can recognize "on sight" a multitude of faces, places, animals, and objects, from a variety of angles, in all kinds of lighting condition, often from only a brief partial glimpse. Despite enormous research efforts and expenditures for over forty years, employing the most sophisticated electronic technology, computers can still scarcely distinguish one face or handwritten letter from another.

This extraordinary yet commonplace human pattern–recognizing ability almost defies analysis. Researchers still do not know exactly how the eye and brain identify letters of the alphabet, let alone entire words or more complex shapes. The majority opinion is that the brain constructs "feature lists," or descriptions of the "significant features" or characteristics of letters, words, faces, and everything else. In a sense, the brain devises a *specification* of what every letter and other object should look like—and then makes decisions on the basis of evidence. "Features" of the object being looked at are checked off on these specifications until a match is found. Recognition then takes place, the result of a perceptual judgment. (The reason prediction is so important in perception is that the more we know about what we might be looking at, the less feature analysis is required to make the identification.)

A feature list is nothing like a photograph or a template stored away in the brain. It has no resemblance to the letter, face, or whatever else it signifies, just as the words and numbers in the specification of a house look nothing like the different buildings that could be constructed to meet its requirements. It is this flexibility that enables us to recognize an object as belonging to a particular category even when we have never seen that object before. Anything that matches the specification is recognized and perceived accordingly—even if we have made a mistake.

But it is not only familiar objects that human beings recognize on sight. Entire landscapes and seascapes, weather patterns, facial expressions, fabrics, the patterns of pieces on chessboards, printed music, maps and diagrams, even moods and intentions, can be identified at a glance. A list of everything our eyes and brain can recognize would be endless.

Then there are all the patterns of *sound* that the brain can recognize "by ear." The feature-analytic theory of visual pattern recognition was itself derived from a theory of acoustic pattern recognition that attempted to account for the complex and subtle human ability to understand speech in all kinds of distorted and noisy conditions. We can also recognize patterns in many other varieties of sounds, in music, rhythms, harmonies, and melodies, in the rustling of leaves, the creaks of a house, even in human and animal footsteps. Once again, no computer comes anywhere near the prodigious human ability to recognize a song or melody from a few notes (often in the middle of the piece, when we switch on the radio). No theorist has any idea how innumerable patterns of sound or sight that are extended *in time* can be represented at any one moment in the architecture of the brain. And then there are all the patterns of smells, tastes, and tactile sensations that we can distinguish, individually and in combination. Think of the different ways in which we can recognize an orange.

And in addition to all the patterns that the human brain can seek and find in time and in space, all the specifications it can construct, there is another vast category of patterns which in a sense exist only as the potential unfolding of experience. I am referring to the brain's ability to recognize distinctive sequences of events and networks of relationships, its gift for understanding and constructing narratives.

The brain is a brilliant, versatile, and incomparable recognizer of patterns in every aspect of life and living, in the actual and the fantastic, in fact and fiction. And it is all accomplished through the two components of imaginative thought that I have already emphasized: (1) the generation of alternative possibilities, of potential specifications and explanations, which I think must be the basic biological predisposition of every brain, our "narrative inheritance," and (2) the selection of the alternatives that best fit our particular purposes and the situation in which we are currently involved. The urge to make such selections must also be innate, but the degree to which such selections will be appropriate, and even our willingness to make them, must obviously be the result of experience. We become skilled because of what life and other people have demonstrated to us.

The Business of the Brain

All the things I have listed are views from different perspectives of one great unsleeping enterprise, the perpetual business of the brain. And the business of the brain is nothing less than the creation of worlds—real, potential, explanatory, and imaginary. Pattern recognition is no different from anything else in my list, though it may be the foundation of them all. Learning can be perceived as the construction and testing of patterns, of specifications, to fit experience. Comprehension is the utilization of those patterns, and remembering is their reconstruction. Reasoning is a matter of moving from one pattern to another, and problem solving the effort to achieve a desired pattern or state of affairs. Imagination is the generation of patterns—and the sharing of them through literature and art. Insight and intuition are the unconscious searching through countless patterns of specifications until an alternative is found that solves the problem, or provides the sought-after clue. The brain lives for narratives, for the construction and experiencing of coherent patterns of events, imposing order on chaos, being on nothingness.

All the things I have discussed must be considered the brain's normal and regular mode of operation, the way it copes with the world and with its own aspirations. None of them are "skills" that require instruction, although all benefit from demonstrations of interesting activities and from collaborative participation in them. If the brain doesn't seem able to do any of the things I have discussed, it must be because something is wrong with the situation, not because of a lack or disability in the individual. To blame children in school for not being able to learn, or comprehend, or think, is like blaming a netfull of fish, stranded on a beach, for not being able to swim.

People are essential for providing the demonstrations and collaboration through which learning naturally occurs. But these "teachers" need not always be present in person. They can be especially effective through *books*. Someone asked me how I developed the passion I have for everything connected with the sea—for boats, voyages, navigation, and the waters themselves, not to mention all the skills and knowledge I've collected related to all of these things. I grew up in a city miles from the open sea, and none of my relatives had any association with seafaring. I had not previously asked myself this question, but I quickly found the answer. The people who introduced me as a youth to the "club of sailors" were Herman Melville and Joseph Conrad. And obviously, there were some other influential teachers who made it possible for me to encounter these authors.

The brain is nourished on narrative. There is no need to instruct it—the brain seeks and produces narratives naturally, whenever it can find the opportunity and the necessary collaboration.

Implications for Education

My conclusion is a simple one. The human brain can be trusted to learn, to comprehend, to think constructively and creatively. The fecundity of the brain has to be recognized and respected by the provision of situations conducive to its productive creativity, situations that are meaningful, relevant, dramatic, and narrative. Children need to let their imaginations roam, through stories, dramatizations, science, play, and art. They must find the pattern of experience their questing brains persistently seek—not just narratives in literature, but in history and geography, in physics and in biology—not only as readers or spectators, but as producers and participants.

Engagement in narrative is a natural activity for the brain. Reading and writing help it to fulfil its most essential purposes. Teachers who use *language* imaginatively—first and second, spoken and written—become the most important persons in a child's development. Teachers can provide the opportunities for the brain to do all those things it naturally does well.

Chapter 2

The Power of Language— First, Second, and Written

Language is commonly regarded as a defining characteristic of human beings. I agree with this, but not for conventional reasons. Explanations usually given for the significance of language to individuals are wrong, I think, and I propose to offer alternative reasons why language is so powerful and compelling for us all, whether as first language, as second language, or as written language.

The reasons most commonly given for the utility of language are that it enables people to communicate needs and feelings and to acquire and exchange information. Language permits us to make pronouncements of this kind without thinking. But a little reflection will quickly show that language is frequently ineffectual for both communicative and informational purposes.

Infants usually communicate and get their needs met perfectly well before they are able to produce and understand speech. Subsequently they are likely to be told to wait or to look after themselves. Statements of need or desire carry no guarantee that they will be accommodated (at which point we may be tempted to revert to more emphatic modes of expression). And language is not very good for describing what we think or how we feel. We may say we are angry, or that we have good intentions, but the words are meager and unreliable representations of our emotions compared with our physical expressions and behavior. For any communication to take place through language, both parties must share not only a common grammar and vocabulary, but common idioms, common expectations, and a common frame of reference. Language could often be considered the antithesis of effective communication—the more words there are, the less mutual understanding there is likely to be. Look at the "communications" of politicians, lawyers, and academics. Language is similarly inadequate as a means of describing and teaching skilled activities, compared with their actual collaborative demonstration.

The word "language" is often regarded as synonymous with "information transmission," but the only kind of information that can easily be acquired, retained, and transmitted through language is *facts*, which proliferate in language and could not exist anywhere else. (Language is required not only to express the "fact" that Brussels is the capital of Belgium, but to establish the relationship in the first place. The two terms, Brussels and the capital of Belgium, are essentially synonymous, each defining the other. Without language, Brussels and Belgium would not even exist as conceptual entities.) Language is largely a closed system; we may learn to move around inside it with great facility, but it is difficult to get beyond it.

We compile immense amounts of information about the world around us and about other people without language. We don't need language to remember how things look, how they sound, smell, or taste, how people behave, and how to get from one place to another. Language is notoriously inferior to films, photographs, maps, graphs, diagrams, flowcharts, spreadsheets, and mathematical symbols as a means of exchanging and representing information about the world. The acquisition of information is a by-product of all forms of experience, not just language. In fact (if only we could control language) I think it would be a good idea to reserve the word "information" for "facts" which exist only in language and to revive the robust, old-fashioned terms *knowledge, belief,* and *understanding* to describe the cognitive consequences of direct interaction with the world and people in it.

I've argued before against the "information processing" metaphor for language (Smith 1983). My response then to the question of what language is good for was "creating worlds," not just the world in which we live, but worlds in which we might or would like to live, and worlds in which we couldn't possibly live, the products of our own and other people's imagination. Stories provide a way of constructing and sharing knowledge of worlds—physical, cultural, and social—and of the roles and relationships of people in them—not by conveying information but by evoking experiences. I intend to delve deeper into how language permits us to enter into different worlds, and in the process to create our own identity.

None of the communicative or informational uses to which language can be put satisfactorily explain why it is universal, why and how we learn it, and why it has such powerful effects on us. The fact that worlds can be created out of language (and that we can communicate about those worlds, for that matter) is hardly a concern of infants who have not yet had a chance to use language for themselves. There must be something much closer to the individual that makes every infant so ready to acquire language, something so powerful that some theorists have proposed that our brains are innately "prewired" to learn language, although of course the actual language and dialect that we learn as "native speakers" out of the many thousands of alternatives cannot be part of our biological inheritance. Infants spend large parts of the first few years of their life learning language, much of which must be totally incomprehensible to them at the beginning. Why do they give it so much attention?

My alternative proposition is that language is *literally* the defining characteristic of human beings. Language provides *definition*—not in the circular sense of supplying words as synonyms for other words, as a dictionary does, but in the ocular sense of providing "focus," a precise shape and structure to experience and to ourselves. The power of language lies in the *identification* that it makes possible—the identification of ourselves, of others, and of the social and cultural worlds we feel part of (or excluded from).

The Power of a First Language

There are two immediate and continuing consequences of learning our first language, which is usually the language of the community into which we are born, our "mother tongue."

The first is that language gives us an *identity card*, a place in the world. The second is that language provides us with a *passport* to further learning through identification with people who know things and can do things. The second consequence of language—the passport—is crucial to our cognitive development and to all other aspects of language use. But it is the first consequence—the identity card—that makes everything possible, including language learning itself.

Establishing an Identity

Our manner of talking establishes for us, and for everyone else, who we are. Children learn to talk like the people they identify with, continuously, effortlessly, and without awareness. The identification begins at birth. In effect, people in the community with which a new baby will be affiliated gather round and say, "Welcome, stranger, you're one of us." And the baby looks up and in effect says, "Hello, friends, I must be just like you." If the people around speak English the infant will learn English. If the people around speak Chinese, the infant will learn Chinese. Whatever the dialect, accent, and idiom of the people around, the infant will come to speak in the same way. The identification will be complete.

I characterize this early language identification as "joining a spoken-language club" (Smith 1988). The benefits are the same as those of any club membership. The first thing that happens after you are admitted is that club activities are revealed to you; you discover the kinds of things members of the club do. When an infant joins a spoken-language club, more experienced members demonstrate the manifold ways in which spoken language is used. They also demonstrate how club members talk. More experienced club members help infants to say what they are trying to say and to understand what they are trying to understand. Everything other club members do is an opportunity for learning, which is usually vicarious, provided the beginner identifies with the other members of the club.

The most immediate consequence of joining any club is the identification—this is who I am, it is where I belong. Affiliation in a club means acceptance on both sides—"Welcome, stranger, you're one of us"; "Greetings, friends, I'm just like you." It is through the many formal and informal clubs that we join in our lifetime—the clubs of particular occupational groups, recreational activities, political allegiances, and personal interests—that we find definition of who we are; we are like the people in the clubs or communities we belong to. We never join a group if we can't identify with its members, if we don't want to, or if its members won't accept us as one of them. We will go to great pains *not* to be identified as members of such groups; we reject those who reject us, and would not want to be mistaken for them.

Learning to talk the way we do is not a matter of imitating models —there is nothing intentional about it. We do what our friends do as a matter of course; we become like them because we see ourselves as being like them. In fact, *trying* to talk the way other people talk when we are not a member of their group is notoriously difficult to do. To a large extent, we can't control the way we talk, not because a habit is ingrained, but because our identity is. We choose our friends, not our language.

The original members of an infant's spoken language club are usually the family—parents, siblings, and their close acquaintances—establishing ties and ways of speaking that may last a lifetime. But many children soon stop talking like their family circle and start talking like people they choose to identify with more closely—they start talking like their friends.

Children don't learn to speak approximately like their friends, they speak *precisely* like them. The outward and tangible manifestation of membership of a community is the way a person talks. Except for a few idiosyncratic pronunciations probably derived from reading, it is usually possible to find a group of people who speak in exactly the same way as an individual whose language is labeled "incorrect." There is nothing *wrong* with the way anyone talks (though something may be considered unacceptable or undesirable about the people they talk like).

Language is the core of our identity. One of the hardest things in the world to change is the way a child talks, for example in the mistaken belief that it will improve the child's chances in life, or "empower" the child. It is also one of the most dangerous things to attempt because it can strip away a child's identity; it is confiscation of the identity card. It is far better to try to provide models that the learner can identify with who speak in other ways. No one is linguistically restricted to membership of just one group, with a single way of talking.

You can't get children to talk like you—unless you can persuade them to identify with you, to see themselves as the same kind of person as you. People don't become teachers or journalists or lawyers because of the way they talk; they talk the way they do because they identify with their colleagues. The language follows the identification.

Very little of this learning is *conscious*—we learn without awareness, just as the people we learn from are unaware that we are emulating them (often in ways they would prefer us not to). We even learn without motivation, sometimes learning things that we would prefer not to learn—mannerisms or attitudes that we would rather do without. In fact, motivation doesn't guarantee learning; we have all experienced frustrating failure to learn something we have wanted desperately to learn, and struggled determinedly to do so.

There is an alternative way of putting all this. Everyone is interested in stories; it is the primary way in which we understand the world, informing ourselves and others of our place and experiences in it (Bruner 1990; Rosen 1986, 1988). One might say that the first concern of all infants is to discover the story of the world into which they are born, and the role that they play in it—whether they have the character of hero, villain, victor, victim, or fool—a role which they then proceed to "act out." And a principal way in which characters are identified in any drama is from the manner of their speech.

Nothing that I have said so far, incidentally, entails that people who have difficulty hearing or speaking must lack an identity. On the contrary, they can acquire a powerful sense of identity through the medium of any fully functioning language in which they can participate, such as the sign language of hearing-impaired people (Sacks 1989).

A Passport for Learning

Language, learning, and thinking advance on a common front. The more language we command—or rather, the more command we have of the languages employed in particular groups or communities—the easier it is to participate in their activities. We think and learn like the people whose language is familiar to us.

If you join the astronomy club, for example, you learn to see yourself as an astronomer and to behave, learn, and think like an astronomer. By helping you to engage in their activities—and in their language—more experienced members of the astronomy club make it possible for you to develop their language and to participate in their knowledge and activities. The astronomical language you command enables you to learn like other members, and to identify more deeply with them. Your language is a passport to entry and to learning in the club.

There are two rather exclusive clubs that cause enormous cognitive and social problems for many students. The first might be called the academic language club, because it is the esoteric language spoken in the educational community. This language seems "natural" or unexceptional to most of us because we are immersed in it all the time, but it is a special language. If you can't tune into this language, it might as well be (it is, in fact) a foreign language. It sounds like English (or whatever the language of instruction might be), but like the languages of many trades and professions, it is a specialized language, with a unique vocabulary and terminology. Familiarity with academic language is essential if students are to succeed or even survive in school—from first grade to graduate school. But not only are many students unacquainted with the language, and confused by it, they are denied the possibility of acquiring familiarity with it and then continuously penalized for not having it.

The second exclusive language, or cluster of languages, requiring extensive command by anyone seeking a place in today's world is the language of literacy. Not only is familiarity with "book language" essential for access to all of the experiences made possible through books, but much spoken language, including that used in the academic club, requires a close acquaintance with literate language.

Unless you command the appropriate language—the relevant ways of talking and thinking—there is no way you can learn as a student or as a reader. There seems to be a catch-22 here. You can't become a member until you are familiar with the language, and you can't learn the language until you join the club. How is it possible to jump on the moving roundabout? Remember that *identification* is the key to club membership and to language learning. The reason we all fail to learn many things is that we cannot identify with experienced members. The reason many students don't learn the language of school is that they don't identify with school, and the real catch-22 is that they are not given the chance.

I have related how the inability of black South African university students to speak and write a brand of English acceptable to white faculty precluded their admission into full membership of the university community—and limited any possibility that their English, their literacy, and their academic skills might improve (Smith 1993). The situation is not dissimilar to that in bilingual education in North America.

Language is a passport to learning. Without the appropriate language, you can't enter the territory, let alone understand what is going on. The appropriate language clears you through immigration control and allows you to receive all the benefits of membership of the community, with other people helping you rather than trying to prevent your admission.

Language also provides a framework on which much of our knowledge, particularly *factual* (often termed "intellectual") knowledge, can be organized. It doesn't mean much to learn that Brussels is the capital of Belgium if you don't know what a capital is, or where Belgium might be, and it is harder to learn and recall the fact as well.

Not all of our learning is through language, of course. Many aspects of our appearance and our habitual behavior can be adopted from other people without the mediation of speech, and language can't do much to facilitate the learning of many skills, from tying shoelaces and riding a bicycle to sailing a boat and programming a computer, beyond general descriptions of procedures and occasional suggestions and warnings.

But without the appropriate language, the ability to learn anything else that is embedded in language is limited. We can only learn what we understand, and if there is a language mismatch, what we might otherwise want and expect to learn can only be confusing. This again is why it can be devastating to try to suppress the way a student talks, in the belief that it will benefit the student or provide entry into desirable communities. In effect, such instructional effort confiscates the passport as well as the identity card. Attempts to empower students, however well-intentioned, may disempower them even further.

The way to give students greater advantages is not by undermining their first language but by augmenting it. Children especially are voracious learners, unintentional mimics, and skilled role-players—provided they have a feeling for the part they are expected or attempting to play. All learners need opportunities to encounter people they can identify with, who can help them to become "members of the club."

The Power of a Second Language

A second language is far more than an additional skill that many people manage to acquire, and it does more than simply consolidate the advantages of a first language. A second language opens up new worlds that often remain completely closed and even unsuspected for unilingual speakers.

A second language expands the intellect, enabling people to break free of a single narrow view. It puts many more visas in their passports to learning. Once it is realized that there is more than one world, the world of a first language, then the possibility of innumerable other worlds and points of view opens up. Monoglots may be unable to venture beyond the confines of their own identity, suffering cultural and cognitive handicaps, especially if they are restricted in their reading.

Mastery of more than one language bolsters the identity with substantial personal and intellectual power, such as the obvious ability to move in cultures and realms of knowledge that other people can't enter. Such unique power may be the reason bilingualism is often taken to be a threat. Someone who is able to use and understand your language and also to converse with other people in a different language may be treated with suspicion, as a spy if not a saboteur. This could be a reason it is often asserted that acquisition of English as a second language should be accompanied by neglect and abandonment of the first language—the ultimate linguistic power play.

Despite frequent assertions, however, second-language competence does not necessarily provide *political* power. Quite the reverse. Individuals who achieve substantial second-language proficiency, or who are on the point of doing so, may continue to be the victims of linguistic discrimination if they themselves are not accepted by the second-language community.

The students in South Africa that I mentioned earlier could often speak three or more of their own African languages fluently, and their *understanding* of English was usually more than adequate. Yet they were held back academically because they had difficulty in meeting arbitrary standards of speaking and writing English. Well-intentioned efforts to teach them English could overwhelm them with mechanical aspects of the language, such as pronunciation, spelling, and punctuation, that would only come with extensive personal experience (not instruction).

Such inadvertent discrimination not only delays competence in English, but can have a catastrophic effect on learning generally. It can severely damage self-esteem and exclude both the opportunities and the confident attitudes necessary for learning in any area.

Parents sometimes refuse to allow their children to speak the first language, in the mistaken idea that it will hold them back. This is an unfortunate misconception because the basis of second-language learning is first-language competence and a strong sense of identity. Demolish the first language and there is no conceptual basis upon which a second language can be established. Diminish the learner's sense of identity, and there is no structure to which a second language can be attached.

Learning a second language presents paradoxical contrasts. It can be effortlessly easy or impossibly difficult, and the difference is not a matter of how motivated you are or how hard you work (or even of the method employed, though any method relying on memorization is bound to be among the worst). It is a question of how easily you are able to join a community of people who speak the second language—how ready you are to identify with them and how open they are to accepting you.

Before formal classroom instruction begins for them, children usually have no problem in making the necessary identification with second-language users, provided they are immersed in the language, participating fully. Such a native ability usually dies the moment there is a conscious attempt to learn a language by memorizing its vocabulary and rules. Unless you already happen to be a successfully polyglot linguist, this is a method that is bound to fail (Krashen 1985), especially as confidence-sapping failing grades come along. The biggest problem is reluctance to immerse oneself in the language—in its sounds and in reading it—the feeling that one *can't* learn the language, that it is too difficult or "foreign."

The worst way to teach a second language is to try to impose it on a learner, especially if the learner is reluctant, uncertain, or in difficulty. The best way is to strengthen the first language and the sense of identity and power that should go with it. The best models for learning a language are those that the learner can identify with—not established members of the dominant language culture (especially if their attitude to bilingualism is disparaging) but members of the learner's own first language community who can demonstrate that second language learning is possible, painless, and worthwhile.

The Power of Written Language

Many theorists have speculated that literacy restructures thought (notably Olson 1994). I'm not sure that the practices of reading and writing necessarily give us different or greater intellectual powers, but they certainly make a difference to us as people. Whether or not we read or write ourselves, the worlds we live in are different because of written language, and our lives are structured by other people's reading and writing practices. The behavior and even the beliefs of everyone are to a large extent controlled by the print in the world. And if we engage in literate practices ourselves, we often can have greater intellectual resources in all of the knowledge and ideas accessible through language that is written.

But a major benefit of literacy is a dramatic extension of the primary power of language, in the establishment and consolidation of our own identity—the way we see ourselves—through access to any community that exists (or has existed or that anyone might imagine existing). And no one has the power to prevent us from identifying with people that we read about. This point is evident in the frequency with which some individuals try to limit access that others might have to books. If they can't prevent experience through reading, they try to limit access to reading.

Our identity is the sum total of all the groups with which we affiliate, and through reading we can be a part of any group in the world. Contrary to a common view, reading is not a solitary activity. I could not begin to list the influential people I have met and the significant events I have participated in through reading, experiences that would have been unattainable for me in any other way. And through writing, we can augment such events ourselves, and venture deeper into relationships that exist exclusively or primarily through written language—in print and on the computer screen.

For many of us, in many ways, literacy has made us what we are. I noted earlier that the way to give students greater advantages is not by undermining their first language but by augmenting it. Their need is to encounter people they can identify with, who will help them to affiliate with alternative or additional communities. By far the most extensive and accessible way to do this is through reading.

The strength of literacy lies not so much in the social, political, and economic advantages that it is supposed to bring—it can often fail to provide these benefits (see Chapter 5 in this book)—but in what it can do for us as individuals. Literacy can help us to find and establish a place in the world, from the strength and purpose that many people find in religious texts to the ideas and inspiration accessible through any library, book or magazine store, or computer network. Countless teachers probably discovered their vocation through youthful identification with a character in a book, actual or fictitious. And many teachers have told me of the support they find for their deepest beliefs about education, despite constant pressures and criticism, in what they read in books. Reading is probably the most widespread subversive practice in the world, and writing can be the boldest, not only in challenging the thought and domination of those in authority, but in providing mutual support and encouragement among those without it.

In addition to contributing so significantly toward the establishment of our identity, literacy can provide many more visas for entry into broad general areas of learning as well as some very specific domains of language. It is worth recapitulating some of the immediate advantages of reading (many of them summarized and substantiated in an important book by Stephen Krashen [1993]).

But before I list some of the learning possibilities that reading provides, I should stress that they are only possible if you are open to seeing yourself as a member of the particular group. You will not be influenced by books about sailing if you can't identify with people who sail or if you have been persuaded, by yourself or someone else, that you will never be a sailor, even in your imagination. And reading won't improve your status as a speller if you have been persuaded, by yourself or by someone else, that spelling is not for you. To make use of the visas that literacy provides, the passport must be valid.

So what are the learning advantages of reading? The first is that you learn to read. Innumerable studies and observations have validated Margaret Meek's insight that the person who teaches children to read is the author of the books that the children read (Meek 1988). And the same applies to older learners as well. The simple and self-evident truth that the more that individuals read, the better readers they become, has frequently been demonstrated in research (Krashen 1993; Nagy, Herman, and Anderson 1985). You don't have to read a lot to become a reader, but the more you read, the better reader you become.

Not only does reading ability improve with the practice of reading, but so does vocabulary, spoken-language expression and understanding, writing ability, spelling and punctuation skills, and general academic competence—provided, once again, that nothing has persuaded you that you can't and don't want to participate. A particular power of literacy is that so much can be accomplished if other people leave learners alone with authors, or at least try not to come between them. Most of our educational problems would go away if only we could allow students to read more, and so, I suspect, would the difficulties many students have concerning their image of themselves.

The Power of Language

To summarize: Without language, we would not be who we are, and the worlds we live in would not be what they are. Language is the source and emblem of our personal identity, and also the passport to our intellectual, social, and political development. All communities and societies of people with common interests have their own language. When we are accepted as a member of a group, we can look any other member in the eye. When we are rejected, or when our language is, we can only turn away.

The manner in which individuals speak is perhaps the principal way in which they are identified, and consequently supported or rejected, embraced or discriminated against. Many people in education recognize the discrimination that language brings, which may lead them to try to change the way some students speak. But language does not guarantee political or social power. People may be discriminated against because of their language, but that does not mean that the discrimination would end if their language were to change. Some other basis would be found for discriminating against them (often on the basis of educational tests).

The role of teachers is not to attempt to inculcate skills but to provide opportunities for personal identification through comprehensible, interesting, and nonthreatening experience. The recurrent question of whether reading should be taught in a first or second language (or alternatively, whether a second language should be taught orally or through reading), loses its point with the realization that language is learned, in all its aspects, through experience rather than through instruction. Students should explore every medium they feel comfortable in; they should talk, listen, read, and write in every language they feel comfortable with.

Teachers must respect language, not as some unattainable ideal of how students ought to speak and write, but as the source of every student's self-image and learning potential. Teachers should also respect the language of the authors of books, a language which gives writers and their creations an identity, which should not be mutilated for the purpose of instruction, evaluation, or political correctness.

And teachers should look into the implications and consequences of the language of their own community, the language of education, with its euphemisms (*special needs, special education, at risk, withdrawal*), evasions (*for the student's good, parents expect it, it's a competitive world out there*), empty mantras (*excellence, standards, challenging*), and ill-considered generalizations (*language is for communication, some people don't speak properly, illiteracy is a disease*).

Language can destroy identities as much as it can construct and reinforce them. No one should be deaf or blind to its power.

Chapter 3

What Happens When You Read?

The question must have been put to me a hundred times in a dozen different ways—*What happens when you read? How do readers read?* or *What is reading?* And I've never found a satisfactory response. But I've never persuaded anyone that the question is not a good one, though I've always had great difficulty understanding what exactly it meant.

Now I want to look at the entire matter in detail, the question and a possible answer. I shall also take the opportunity to discuss a pair of related recurrent questions, *What is comprehension?* and that venerable chestnut, *What is meaning?*

Philosophers have long speculated about meaning and understanding from an abstract point of view, producing interminable theorizations but no resolutions. Scientists test models of hypothetical underlying processes on computers or under rigidly controlled experimental conditions. Teachers ask the questions for practical reasons, for example to gain insight into how they might better teach reading or writing. It is the practical approach that I want to take. Philosophical and scientific hypotheses interest us all, but when it comes to the here and now of helping people to read and write, it is better to avoid metaphysical brambles and find a pathway that will keep us moving forward.

The question of what it means to read came up most recently for me from a writer's point of view, at a seminar for newspaper journalists. An experienced editor pointed to a newspaper on the table in front of us, tapped the lead article authoritatively several times, and demanded, "So, what happens when you read that news story? How *do* readers read?" He seemed confident that "experts" should have an answer to such a simple inquiry. After all, that was the reason for the seminar—for academic researchers and theorists to enlighten journalists on the state of the art in the study of reading.

I could have talked about eye movements, but I didn't think that was what the questioner was interested in. Eye movements bear about as much relation to what happens when we read as knife and fork movements do to digestion; they are conspicuous, but give little indication of what is going on inside. I could have expounded on transforming printed letters and words into internalized sounds, but I think *that* theory of reading is wrong. And in any case, it is not an answer, any more than listening to a story or anecdote could be explained by saying that we hear the words. I could have mentioned acquiring information from text, but I have never understood the compulsion we are all supposed to have for collecting information. I could have talked about activating memories and constructing meaning, but I didn't think jargon would contribute to understanding.

Other academic participants in the seminar didn't share my qualms. They replied that readers read by activating memories and constructing meaning. Astonishingly—to me—the questioner seemed satisfied with this response. He wrote it on his notepad. Was this the enlightenment that he was seeking? Was this *news* to a newsman—that reading involves knowledge and comprehension? Did he think it might be otherwise?

Obviously, he must have drawn something from these responses. Perhaps they focussed his mind on matters that writers should never forget—that readers benefit when the text helps them to revive relevant memories and to make sense of what the writer is trying to say. But didn't the editor know these things already? Why was he asking the question?

I asked him why he was asking the question. Now *he* was baffled. Why should I ask that? Wasn't it a clear and reasonable question? Surely experts had something enlightening to say about reading. He repeated the question more emphatically, just to help me out. "What do *you* think happens when you read?"

I thought for a moment and said, "An experience takes place." That was the best answer I could offer at the time, though my questioner seemed to find it lacking in force and profundity. "What kind of experience?" he asked—and there he had me. Perhaps now, with the advantage of time for reflection and writing, I can explain myself a little better.

The Experience of Experience

I suspect that my terse response was triggered by recollection of Louise Rosenblatt's distinction between reading to acquire information and reading for the experience of reading itself. She has argued that reading for experience is either ignored in educational situations or else totally confounded with reading for information (Rosenblatt 1978, 1980). My view is that we acquire information *only* when we are reading for experience, unless we deliberately try to memorize parts of the text, a futile as well as unappealing procedure. Anything read simply to be memorized is learned as nonsense, recalled as nonsense, and rapidly forgotten. To make sense of what we read we have to read for experience—or rather, reading has to *be* an experience—and memories automatically follow.

We remember what we make sense of (unless we remember an experience of not making sense of something). Information acquisition is a by-product of experience, whether we are reading or engaging in any other kind of activity. We always "acquire information"—we remember things—as a consequence of experience. We remember the things that were the most surprising or interesting to us, that we were most involved in. We don't live for information, we live for experience. And what we remember is usually in the form of a story, a story of "what happened" to us or to someone else with whom we can identify, or at least empathize. Any "facts" (or "information") that we remember are usually part of those stories.

A Pedestrian Analogy

Suppose that instead of "What happens when you read?" the question had been "What happens when you walk?" Once again, a response might be framed at various levels—from "your legs move" to all kinds of complex physical and neurological analyses. But suppose the questioner then said, "I know all that. What I mean is: what happens when people walk along a beach, or in the woods, or through a shopping mall?"

An "information" point of view might say that we walk to achieve an objective, to "get somewhere." But the reason for walking could be the activity itself, not the destination, which is often the same as the starting point. And even if we do reach a destination, things happen while we walk that attract our attention; we may look out for certain things, but others come spontaneously to mind. There is no way to specify *everything* that might happen when we walk, or even to make a comprehensive summary. We have *experience* while we walk—that's all that can be said in answer to such a general question. And usually we can remember something from the walk. Certain aspects of the journey and of our feelings remain with us, for a long time if they are particularly unusual or significant to us. That is the "information" that we inevitably acquire as a result of experience.

Of course, our mind may wander as we walk. We may not remember much of the ground we have covered, and may even forget the reason we started out, if we had a reason apart from "going for a walk." So too with reading. No two people experience anything in the same way, especially not a text; how could they? And no two sets of memories will be the same, though most people might tend to remember events that are particularly distinctive or dramatic.

The Reading Experience

But how do printed words become experience? Isn't something extra, something *special*, taking place when we read? Don't we have to identify individual words first, and somehow persuade ourselves that these words describe or represent a different state of affairs, and not just ink-marks on paper, before we can experience something from reading?

How is any situation transformed into an experience? Not by our identifying particular elements of the situation we are in and then combining them into something whole and meaningful. The identification of elements comes after the experience, as a consequence rather than a cause. Before we have some grasp of the experience, its elements would be meaningless. That does not mean that experience does not develop and change over time; the change may sometimes be dramatic. But experience supervenes from the beginning of any event in which we are involved. We see a figure lurking in some trees, and our experience is one of uncertainty. The experience changes when we recognize a friend exercising his dog.

Print before it becomes part of a reader's experience is meaningless; nothing can be done with it. Normally when we read a story, a poem, a newspaper article, or an interesting argument, our experience carries us along. The experience invariably changes as we read—as it does when we walk—but it cannot stop. If all experience from reading ended, reading would stop, even though our gaze might still be fixed to the page. We would have run into a mental brick wall.

A different analogy may help to demonstrate how something in print can become an immediate part of experience.

Imagine an "actual" event, something that is "really happening" to you. It is night and you are on a camping expedition, snug in your sleeping bag. You are abruptly awakened by a rustling sound, and sense that something large is moving about outside. You sit up and look around. Moonlight casts vague shadows on the tent walls. You cautiously feel for your flashlight but can't find it. For one long silent moment you suspect you might have been dreaming. Then distinctly and unmistakably you hear a muffled succession of plods, more shuffles than steps, moving purposefully toward your side of the tent. A larger shadow looms, and an ungainly hulk stumbles against the wall beside you. The taut canvas sways. Huge nails rasp down the tent inches from your head, and cold air blows in. The tent is ripped again, and a terrifying . . .

Need I go on? If you had been in that situation, what could you say happened to you—not outside you, outside the tent, but *inside* you, as the events unfolded? What could you say except that you had a frightening experience—a rapidly developing turmoil of thoughts and emotions? You could say that the noises mystified you and that subsequent events terrified you. But your mental tumult and physical reactions did not cause the experience, they *were* the experience.

All you can say when you are involved in *any* situation is that you have an experience. The experience is your involvement. It is immediate, unpremeditated, and compelling. It just *happens*. You can describe many different kinds of experience, but you can't describe or explain "experience" itself. To explain experience, you would have to analyze innumerable distinct experiences.

Now suppose you were watching a movie of the incident I have just described. What would happen to you? Once again you would have an experience, involving mental and emotional reactions probably little different from those you would have had in the actual event. You might not suffer the physical injuries that the actual situation threatened, but you would probably be totally immersed in the situation itself. If the scene was as compelling as many movie episodes are, you would be unable to remain uninvolved. Even if you closed your eyes, the soundtrack would keep you involved. Your emotional reactions might even be enhanced. The idea that going to the theatre involves a "willing suspension of disbelief" does not apply unless the play or movie is truly awful; the usual situation is that we are unable to suspend *belief*. We may try to tell ourselves these are only actors, or shadows on a screen, and that we are safe and secure in our own living room or with a hundred other people in a theatre—but we don't believe it if we are caught up in the drama.

There are no intermediate steps in any of this. You don't analyze elements of a theatrical situation in order to have an experience, any more than you do for an "actual" situation. Both situations are in fact "actual." You are involved in both. If you like, you can say that the movie "fools you" into believing the situation is real, but in fact you fool yourself, in responding to it as if it were real. In both circumstances, the "actual" and the "representational," you had experiences, and to a large extent these experiences were mentally and emotionally identical. The movie is not, I would argue, a "representation" of a reality, actual or imagined. The movie *is* reality—the reality you are experiencing at the time you are watching it.

Now, finally, what happens when you read? May I remind you that you *have been* reading. Reflect upon what happened when you read my description of the night-in-the-tent situation—deliberately written, I should confess, to try to create a particular experience for readers. If I was indeed able to involve you in the situation as a reader, then your experience would have been similar to that of viewing the movie or being in the "actual" situation. Stories, spoken or written, extended or episodic, do not *represent* realities; they *are* realities in their own right. We don't respond to the words or information that we derive from the print; we respond to the print. We can't tell ourselves "this is only print" any more than we can tell ourselves "this is only a movie." If we are involved, then we have the experience, immediately and inexorably.

Physiologically, it is all the same behind the eyeballs and the ear drums. We may *think* (or try to tell ourselves) that we are participating in an actual situation, or watching a movie, or reading printed words on paper, but the neural impulses that pass to the brain from the eyes and ears on different occasions are indistinguishable in kind. "Images" do not pass to the brain from the eyes, nor sounds from the ears. If brain researchers were able to tap into the neural activities in the optic nerve, they would be unable to distinguish whether the individual was being threatened by a real bear or reading about an imaginary one. If we experience events as visual or auditory, imagined or real, it is because we label them in particular ways. We can't involve ourselves in a novel or a poem *and* constantly remind ourselves that we are reading a novel or poem; the experience requires *ignoring* that we are reading. After the event, if we notice the fact at all, we *remember* that we were reading. Otherwise we are likely to think that our experience was "real."

I don't know if the one-track physiology of the visual system is the total reason reading experiences are as real to us as any other kind. The brain may be evolutionarily incapable of distinguishing "representations" from "actual" events. Until human beings started telling each other stories, or drawing each other pictures, the only kind of reality around was "real" reality, whatever the physical world was doing. Now through various arts and technologies we have multiple ways of constructing or representing realities, although the brain still has only one way of responding to human artifacts—as real. Whatever the explanation, we can only respond to any situation in which we are involved—to any experience—as "real." If we want to react to or remember an occurrence as fiction, as a human construction of some kind, then we have to attach a mental tag to it, reminding ourselves that it is "not real"—a label which is often not very effective or long-lasting.

How does it happen? What is the chemistry by which print on the page become experience inside us? I don't think anyone knows the answer, any more than anyone knows how an external event becomes an internal experience. Philosophers and psychologists have invented all kinds of "mediating structures" inside us that are supposed to convert a charging rhinoceros, or a story of a charging rhinoceros, into palpitations of the heart, but no one has been able to lay out a map or circuit diagram with all the connections and interactions. Experts in various disciplines may talk as if it has all been put together, or as if they know how to put it together, but it hasn't, and they don't. I feel secure on my ground when I argue that our experiences of the "real" and of the fictitious are the same, but I don't know of a single scientist I could call on to explain or refute why this should be the case.

All fictions are realities, and many of our realities may be fictions (maybe all, but I don't want to get lost in a metaphysical maze). It is for these reasons that I have had to be so profligate with quotation marks around such terms as "actual" and "real" in this chapter. I would not want to have to define the terms or to defend my use of them. I want to give them their usual uncomplicated role in common sense discourse, but at the same time indicate that their use is philosophically question-able indeed. I am writing with my analytical fingers crossed. Perhaps I can give up the quotation marks from now on.

What happens when we read? We are engaged in an experience—real, immediate, and irresistible. What do we have experience of? What-ever circumstances the text involves us in. What is the nature of that experience? Much the same as it would be if we were involved in those circumstances in any other way.

The Question Rephrased

When I gave my tentative and succinct answer to the editor, he mur-mured noncommittal remarks like "hmmm," "interesting," and "I'll think about it." He was a generous and open-minded person.

Later he made his question a little more precise. What he really wanted to know, he said, was what gets readers over the jump. That's journalistic jargon for a page turn, the point where a story starting on one page is continued on another. Instead of asking, "What happens when you read?" he was now asking "What keeps you reading?" And once again I think there is a simple one-word answer which he undoubt-edly knew already: interest.

On reflection I don't think that answer is totally true. Sometimes sheer determination can keep us reading, or trying to read, something that doesn't interest us very much. Some readers will keep on reading because they are addicted; they can hardly spend a moment not indulg-ing their habit.

But writers can't rely on perverse or neurotic conditions to keep their readers reading. There is only one thing writers can count on to do the trick, and that is to make the story they are telling comprehensible and interesting. They must make reading the story an interesting experience. I don't intend to try to define what experience is, and I certainly don't plan to explicate interest. Everyone knows what interest is, don't they? Teachers and writers certainly ought to.

Every teacher should be able to recognize interest or lack of interest on the part of students—it is written on their faces. Anything that isn't interesting is boring or confusing, and no one can easily disguise those conditions. Writers may not be able to see the faces of their readers, but part of their stock-in-trade should be knowledge of what their intended readers would be likely to find interesting, and how to write interestingly. There are no formulae for these things that experts can provide. I don't expect that a Nobel prize will ever be awarded for a cure for tedious writing.

I can offer a homespun synonym for interest—*involvement*, the word I have been using as the essence of experience. Readers keep reading, they go "over the jump," when they are involved in what they are reading, having an experience they want to prolong. As for any question of how to write interestingly, journalists should know more about that than reading researchers, and they shouldn't feel they have to ask them.

On Undefinable Words

When I try to explain reading, and so much else, with reference to experience, the next question is often, *What do you mean by experience?* This surprises me, since I would think everyone is familiar with the word, and I'm not trying to use it in any esoteric or recondite way. Some carping critics even ask me to define the word. I don't think they ask me through ignorance—it is an argumentative ploy.

The dictionary doesn't offer a definition of experience, but merely some approximate paraphrases and examples of the word's use, such as personal knowledge, a state of mind, and "what we are conscious of." I doubt if anyone questioning that reading was experience would be satisfied if I said reading was a state of mind. The trouble is not that I'm being deliberately uncooperative in refusing to define experience, and neither is the dictionary. The trouble is that the word is undefinable.

Real, reality, and *actual* are other examples of perfectly good words that can't be defined, although we usually know what they mean in context. We can even say what some of their opposites are—false is (sometimes) the opposite of real, fantasy is (sometimes) the opposite of reality, potential is (sometimes) the opposite of actual, ignorance (or innocence, or unconsciousness) is the opposite of experience. Words that are common currency in everyday discourse become intractable when philosophers and psychologists get hold of them and gravely ask what they *mean* (or worse, what they "really" mean).

The simple reason why words like reality and experience cannot be defined, or even described, is that they are as far as you can go. They may explain other words, but are themselves the fundamental condition, the bottom line, the basic form, postulatory, axiomatic. You cannot go deeper (the way you can by defining a dog as a mammal or as an animal); you can only go sideways, by describing different kinds of experience the way you might list different breeds of dog, except that the variety of possible experiences is infinite.

A contemporary French philosopher, Clement Rosset (1989), puts the case with exemplary clarity and simplicity, in a lucid translation, in an article entitled "Reality and the Untheorizable." He says that reality is what we live in—it couldn't be anything else. Reality is everything that happens to us and that could happen to us. If reality were any different, it would be a different reality. It is too immediate, too close to us, too changeable, ever to allow us a vantage point from which to survey it objectively. We can describe what *our* reality is at any time, or what we would want it to be, but we can't say what reality *is*.

The same with experience. It is what happens to us, what we see, think, and feel at any moment. It is personal, amorphous, changing from moment to moment. We can always describe *an* experience—but never experience itself.

What is the experience of reading? It is whatever reading does to you. Its essence cannot be captured. Read about a shipwreck and you have the experience of a shipwreck, possibly diluted in some respects but probably elaborated in others. Read about a political theory and you have the experience of encountering, reacting to, and reflecting upon a set of political ideas. The experience is whatever engages your attention, whatever you think about.

Let me throw a couple of other commonly complicated words into the hopper at this point—*comprehension* and *meaning*.

On Comprehending Comprehension

There is a powerful feeling among many educators and researchers that there must be some mediating inner procedure in reading between the text and the experience, or between the text and recollection. That additional factor is usually termed *comprehension*, regarded as a "process" that takes place after the printed words are identified but before reading is complete. Some theorists and producers of educational materials even talk about "comprehension skills" which learners are supposed to have in order to read and which they may lack if they experience particular difficulties in "understanding." But comprehension is not a set of skills—or if it is, it is one that we have all had from birth. The opposite of comprehension is not ignorance, but confusion. Comprehension is a state, part of every experience.

Once again, there is no point in asking what comprehension really is, as though it is a process—or even a state—that can be described. It is possible to offer general descriptions of what an absence of comprehension might entail, like feelings of confusion, uncertainty, and inadequacy, but it is not so easy to explain what comprehension feels like. It is like breathing—we are usually only aware of it when it is difficult. Comprehension is our normal state of mind. Like reality and experience, it is simply *there*. It is not a difficult word to use, only to define.

A particular problem with the word comprehension is that it is often used to mean "interpretation," and that is another matter. Comprehension can't be challenged, but interpretation can. The way we comprehend something is just that: we comprehend. I can't disagree with your comprehension, or say that it is right or wrong. That would be like disagreeing with your consciousness, or denying that you had an experience. But we can disagree with each other's interpretation. Teachers can say that a student's interpretation of a text is not the same as theirs, and that it is certainly not the way the text ought to be interpreted. But interpretations are notoriously subjective and frequently ideological; they depend on beliefs and experience, not on skill. Interpretation can't be taught, but interpretations can. The same applies to interest, and interests.

On the Meaning of Meaning

Questions about the meaning of meaning could be the most paradoxical ever asked, because you must presumably know the answer before being able to ask the question. If you don't know what meaning means, how can you ask the meaning of meaning? Nevertheless at least one book has been written with precisely that title, and philosophers and psychologists have struggled with the question for centuries.

The reason, I would again suggest, is that a perfectly good word has been treated as if it referred to something substantial and tangible in its own right. I can ask if you mean what you say, or what you mean by what you say. I can ask if something means the same to you as it does to me, or what you think the meaning is of something that you read. But I should not ask you what meaning itself is. It is another undefinable word.

Even if I did give you an answer—and there has never been a shortage of public-spirited individuals ready to do just that—what could you do with it? Suppose I told you that meaning was the metaphysical prototype of terrestrial shadows, as some philosophers have claimed. Would that help you teach reading? Suppose, like some linguists and cognitive psychologists, I told you that meaning was an inner paraphrase in propositional form of the semantic elements of a statement. Would that make you a better writer? Perhaps when someone asks what meaning (or reality, or experience, or comprehension) means, they should declare what kind of an answer would help them.

There is no point in looking for something inside someone, some physiological or psychological structure, to be, reflect, or represent meaning. Meaning is not that kind of thing; it is more like an experience than an entity. We don't need trees inside ourselves to recognize trees, and we don't need meanings inside ourselves to comprehend meanings. We only confuse ourselves looking for inner correlates of words that actually refer to states and relationships.

A final point. Rather than discussing the meaning of meaning, perhaps it would be better to ask what the meaning of the meaning of meaning might be. What could anyone mean by the meaning of meaning? Can there be superordinate and subordinate meanings, or would such statements be as meaningless as references to the taste of a taste or the height of a height?

I hope the previous paragraph was incomprehensible. It was intended to be. I wanted to illustrate a psychological phenomenon called *saturation*, which occurs when any word, however sensible it might usually be, is endlessly repeated. Say your own name to yourself often enough and it becomes just a sequence of meaningless sounds. This, I suspect, is what happens with the word "meaning." In some academic contexts it is used so frequently, with such intensity, that it loses meaning altogether. The problem with many of the key words and phrases that puzzle teachers—and writers—is simply that we hear them so often, in such inappropriate yet portentous contexts, that they become nonsensical to us. We forget that they make sense.

What Teachers (and Writers) Might Do with the Answer

I suppose there is an implication behind my response to the editor's question about reading, and that is that there is nothing to be known. There is no need to ask the question, or at least to worry about it, because there is no mystery (beyond the essential mystery of how a soggy bundle of neural interconnections inside the skull is able to generate feelings of any kind of experience at all). Nothing goes on in the back room of the brain that writers (or teachers) need take into account in their work. When you write, don't think of the brain of the reader— think of the reader. When you teach reading, don't think of the brain of the student—think of the student.

Could my journalistic interrogator have truly thought that science, even "at the cutting edge," would have something of great illumination to say about reading and writing, something he did not know despite his years of professional experience? Many teachers have such a faith. They have been persuaded that there is a *science of reading* that knows more about teaching and reading than they do.

Science is a fascinating and important pursuit in many of its aspects. But there are situations in which science is not relevant—or at least, where it still has to make a case for its relevance. The "scientific study of reading" contributes more to theoretical attempts to elucidate physiological mechanisms behind thought and behavior than to specific issues of how to teach or write effectively. When researchers or theorists make "scientific" pronouncements on education, which many are not reluctant to do, they can do so in condescending ways that give little credit to the insights of teachers or writers. But if you are having trouble with what you are trying to teach or to communicate, the problem is much less likely to lie in ignorance of the detailed way the human brain functions than in your general understanding of the feelings and thoughts of the particular individual you are trying to reach.

To improve the way you communicate with someone, whether through writing or teaching (or both), you should consider the state of the recipient. Is the person likely to be confused, bored, overwhelmed, intimidated, angered, or resentful? What kind of experience is this person likely to be having, either as a reader or as a learner?

The answer will not be found by consulting an expert or a dictionary, but by trying to teach or write better. To do this you observe the person (or kind of person) you are trying to reach, and you study how other people do what you are trying to do, especially if they appear able to do it well. In other words, if you are a writer you *read*—you immerse yourself in the way other people do what you are trying to do. And if you are a teacher, you observe and reflect upon the way *you* and people around you learn, and the kinds of behavior and circumstance that facilitate such learning.

We learn from each other. And that, I finally suspect, might have been my canny editor's intention. When he challenged researchers to say what happens when we read, what he "really meant" was, could we say anything *relevant* to a practical situation? Could we make explicit what he obviously knew from his years of journalistic experience—that the way to hold a reader is to tell an interesting and coherent story? What happens when you read that keeps you reading? I have an expanded answer now. You get something to think about.

Chapter 4

Learning to Read: The Never-Ending Debate

Controversy over reading instruction flares with predictable regularity, almost as soon as the smoke and passion of the previous outbreak have subsided. Teachers are once more being reproached for failure to make children literate. They are urged to stop using the wrong method or to concentrate on using the right method of teaching children to read. And the controversy is as pointless today as it always has been because it is based on a misconception about how children learn and how teachers teach.

The debate is currently bringing into vehement opposition two views about how reading should be taught, widely known as the *phonics* (or "skills," or "basics") approach, and the *whole language* (or "naturalistic," "emergent literacy," or "literature-based") philosophy. I shall discuss both views, how they arose, why they are in such conflict, and why the issue of "which is right" can never be satisfactorily resolved. But first I want to look at the more basic question of how children learn to read—indeed how they learn anything. We must begin by acknowledging that there are conflicting views about how learning takes place.

Two Views of Learning

The prevailing view in education today is that learning is usually difficult and takes place sporadically, in small amounts, when properly organized and rewarded, as a result of solitary individual effort. Students must have a deliberate intention to learn and must give learning their full and (if necessary) repeated attention. Some people are better at learning than others, although anything can be learned if attempted often enough, at an appropriate level, and with sufficient "desire" and adequate reinforcement. Learning is transient, and most of what is learned is likely to be quickly forgotten unless "rehearsed" or "refreshed"—especially before examinations and tests.

This view of learning is what most teachers are taught, indeed it is *how* many of them are taught; they are given the facts and expected to memorize them. I call this the *official* view of learning, because it prevails almost universally in education. The official view is also widespread in the general population. Most people have come to believe that learning is difficult and requires effort. They look upon it as *work*.

But there is an alternative view of learning that is at least two thousand years old, and well known, as far as I can discover, in every culture of the world. It is a commonplace view for everyone outside education—and even for most educators when they are off duty. I call it the *informal* view. This view is that learning is continuous, spontaneous, and effortless, requiring no particular attention, conscious motivation, or specific reinforcement. It occurs in all kinds of situations, and is not subject to forgetting. In this view, learning is social rather than solitary. It can be summarized in seven familiar words: *We learn from the company we keep.*

The official and the informal views of learning are opposed in almost every respect. It is surprising that so many people can keep both views in their head at the same time. Possibly they store them in different sides of their brain. The two views of learning are so contradictory that they would appear to refer to two entirely different kinds of learning, or even two entirely different kinds of mental activity. The official view looks at learning as *memorization*, while the informal view regards it as *growth*. I shall examine the informal view first.

The Informal View

That we learn from the company we keep is common, everyday wisdom. Every parent knows that children learn to talk exactly like their friends, and to dress and behave exactly like their friends, and to perceive the world in exactly the same ways their friends do. It is impossible to prevent them from doing so. No matter how much of the day children hear their parents or their teachers talking, they will not learn to talk as their parents or teachers talk, at least not as long as they see themselves as being more like their friends than like their parents and teachers.

Children don't talk as they do through ignorance, or through lack of instruction. In fact they can't be *instructed* to talk in other ways. They talk and dress and see the world the way their friends do because they see themselves as the same kind of people as their friends. They have not learned a set of facts or skills; they have acquired an identity. To try through instruction and exhortation to change the way children talk or behave is to try to change their identities, the way they see themselves. It should not be surprising that attempts to *make* children behave in ways contrary to how they see themselves can be so unavailing and stressful for all concerned. Teaching depends on helping students to develop their images of themselves. It can only be done successfully with considerable patience and sensitivity—the acme of a teacher's art.

We all know that children grow to be like the company they keep, that is why parents are so concerned about their children's friends. We know that this learning is effortless, unconscious, and continuous. I have never heard a parent—even a parent who is a teacher—say, "I don't worry about the gang that my son hangs out with; he's a slow learner." We inspect the schools that our children might attend, knowing that young people will almost certainly finish up like the friends they make in school. Their identity is at stake. We all join clubs and other formal and informal associations because they are made up of people we see ourselves as being like, or would like to be like. I have characterized this coming to be like the company we keep as "joining the club" (Smith 1988). Children learn to talk through their membership in the "spoken language clubs" made up of the people they will come to talk like: first family, then friends. And children learn to read and write if they join the "literacy club," literally identifying themselves with people who read and write.

In other words, learning is social and developmental. We grow to be like the people we see ourselves as being like. Learning is therefore also a matter of identity, of how we see ourselves—but our identity is determined for us socially as well. We learn who we are from the way others treat us. The learning is *vicarious*; it is not a consequence of instruction and practice but of demonstration and collaboration. We learn from the people who interest us and help us to do the things they do. We often refer informally to people who have been significant influences on our lives—helping to make us the person we are today—as our "teachers," whether or not we met them in the classroom. The verb "to teach" originally meant "to show." That is what effective teachers do: they demonstrate what can be done (and their own attitude toward what can be done), and they help others to do it. They make newcomers members of clubs to which they themselves belong.

Tremendous but unsuspected amounts of learning are accomplished in this way, far more than anyone could adequately outline. Four-year-olds learn about twenty new words a day. By the time they enter school they know around ten thousand words. They don't all know the same ten thousand words, of course, but they know most of the ten thousand words their friends know. They don't know all the words their teachers know, but they may know words their teachers don't know.

By the time they leave school they know at least fifty thousand words; maybe ten times that number (depending, not surprisingly, on how much reading they do). They are familiar with several grammars—the grammars used by the people they identify with (in the real world and on television), all different from the formal grammar taught in classrooms. They learn all kinds of linguistic complexity—intricate intonation patterns, formal and informal registers of speech, and a multitude of idioms. They learn with great subtlety and precision how to present themselves to the world: how to behave, to react, and to express themselves (as the kind of person they learn they are). They learn values, relationships, and attitudes, positive and negative. They learn whether they are regarded as readers and writers. They learn who they are, who they might become, and who they are unlikely ever to become.

This unconscious, continual, and effortless learning goes on throughout life. And it is all achieved without a "method." Social interactions bring about the growth of learning.

This continual development of complex understanding and abilities is so different from our typical struggles to learn in educational contexts that it is sometimes regarded not as learning, but as "imitation" or even as the manifestation of something innate, something already a part of us. Some researchers, astounded by the rapidity and scope of children's language development, have concluded that language is part of our biological inheritance. But our genes do not determine which particular dialect of the more than three thousand natural languages in the world we will master—the people we identify with do. We don't talk as our ancestors did, but like the company we keep today. And we never forget who we are, even when we make consciously deliberate decisions to change our behavior or our perceptions of ourselves. What we learn from the company we keep stays with us through life.

The Official View

So why is the official view of learning so radically different from the informal view?

When experimental psychologists began studying learning just over a hundred years ago, they didn't look at what was learned by people in the communities in which they lived. That wasn't regarded as "scientific"; it was in the province of anthropologists, not experimentalists. Psychologists restricted themselves to the study of learning in the laboratory, in situations that could be experimentally manipulated and controlled. They didn't look at how people learned the things that interested them or made sense to them, though this is the way learning takes place outside the laboratory. Interest and past experience were regarded as "extraneous variables" that "contaminated" experiments and interfered with statistical reliability and replicability. Instead the experimenters looked at how individuals learned nonsense in isolated conditions wholly contrived by the experimenter. Learning nonsense was and still is termed "pure learning."

In a typical learning experiment, subjects are seated in rows in a room sealed off from the outside world, warned not to help each other, and given a list of about a dozen nonsense items to study—syllables or sequences of digits that make no sense to them. The experimenter carefully records how long it takes each subject to commit the items on the list to memory, and the subjects are required to return several days later to see how many items they can recall. And if the subject can remember only a few of the items, the score-keeping experimenter might say, "You didn't learn very much, did you?" No attention is paid to all the informal learning accomplished by the subject, such as what the experimenter looked like, how the room was furnished, how difficult and boring the task was, and the fact that the subject "didn't learn very much." Yet these are matters that a person may well remember for life. The fact that repetition and effort facilitate the memorization of nonsense became established as a fundamental "law of learning."

This became the *official* theory of learning—because it was scientific, controlled, and dependable. Everyone learned nonsense in the same way, and the learning could be guaranteed, provided enough time was spent "on task." If a person did not learn everything the first time, the material was to be presented again and again. Incidentally, the experimentalists also discovered a less well-publicized "law of forgetting": subjects start to forget the meaningless items they have memorized from the lists (though not what they learned informally from the experimental situation) immediately after the last learning trial.

And education adopted the official theory of learning lock, stock, and barrel. (The law of forgetting was forgotten.) Suddenly, classrooms became like experimental laboratories. Learning became a matter of individual effort, students were required to memorize items on lists, teachers started keeping scores, collaboration became cheating—and those students whose test results were low were told they hadn't learned very much. And teachers were blamed for not having taught those students very well. I have recounted in *Joining the Literacy Club* (1988) the whole sorry story of "how education backed the wrong horse" when it put its money on experimental psychology's theory of learning.

What students actually learn in school is usually ignored; all the attention is given to what they fail to memorize. This is why so much assessment is required: only "tests" will uncover how much nonsense individuals have succeeded in temporarily assimilating. What students actually and inevitably *learn*—their feelings about the utility and attainability of what they are taught and about their teachers and themselves—is there for anyone to see, but it receives no attention until a student is diagnosed as having learning problems or special needs.

Learning to Read

If children learn from the company they keep, how do they learn to read? To answer this question, there is no point in looking for evidence from the experimental laboratory or from educational statistics. It is irrelevant to consider how children struggle through classroom exercises in reading instruction. Instead, we should look at how they come to terms with printed language.

There is massive evidence (Goelman, Oberg, and Smith 1984) that two groups of people—two kinds of company—together ensure that children learn to read. The first group is the people who read to children—the parents, the siblings and friends, and above all the teachers—who do so much to determine whether a child makes the crucial step of "joining the literacy club." The second group is the authors of the books that children love to read.

The simple act of reading to children serves a multiplicity of vital purposes. It puts the children in the company of people who read, shows them what can be done with reading, sparks their interest in the consequences of reading, informs them about the nature of stories, and—most important—it puts them in the company of authors. The role of teachers is critical; they need great skill and insight. Teachers must find material for every individual child in their classroom to be interested in, ensuring that each child is helped to read and protected from boredom, anxiety, and failure (all matters that distant instructional designers and educational planners cannot attend to). And the culminating responsibility of teachers is to hand each child over to authors.

The phrase "reading to children" is somewhat misleading and has caused some people to fear that it will encourage children to be passive and dependent. But anyone who has ever read to children knows that a child, even an infant, is rarely passive. Children read *with* the adult as much as they can (they want to look at the book too), eventually turning the page before the adult is ready in order to get on with the story. Children are too independent—and too impatient—to allow adults to read for them when they can read for themselves. A much better phrase than "reading to children" might be "helping children to read." This phrase would clarify how authors become the company that actually teaches a child to read.

Margaret Meek (1988) has documented exactly how authors teach reading. She emphasizes that the books must be those that children know well—the favorite stories that they know by heart or the predictable stories in which it is obvious what a word will be before it is actually encountered. That prior knowledge is the point, according to Meek. The child already knows the words, and *the author shows the child how to read them*. The author, essentially, takes over as the person helping the child to read.

The authors of books that children read make several vital contributions, some of which only authors can make. They help children to recognize written words. This is no more complex for children than learning to recognize the sounds and meanings of spoken words, twenty words a day, and it progresses even faster. The more written words that children are able to recognize, the easier it is for them to understand and learn new words. Authors also teach the meanings of words. Much literate adult vocabulary comes from reading—not from looking up words in dictionaries but from comprehending their meaning from the context in which they appear.

Authors have the advantage of being infinitely patient and tolerant collaborators. A parent or teacher draws the line at reading the same passage six times in a row, but this does not bother an author. Authors don't mind if readers skip difficult or boring passages, and they have no temptation to bring a child to order every time a mistake is made or attention wanders. Authors give children *control*, the power to read as they want rather than as a teacher expects. They give children the competence and confidence to tackle the more difficult—and sometimes more boring—material that they will encounter elsewhere in their educational life.

This leads to another advantage that authors possess: they make children secure as members of the reading club. Children who read independently *know* they are engaging in powerful behavior. And a final unique role that authors play is providing access to every other club in the world. How many teachers entered their profession because the stories they read about teaching enabled them to see themselves in that role?

In asserting that children learn to read by reading, it may sound as if I am disproving my argument that learning is a social activity. But readers keep company with the authors that they read, and also with the characters in the stories that are read. Reading enables many people—including many children—to escape solitude. Readers are never alone.

Theories of Teaching Reading

The Seductiveness of Phonics

For as long as there have been records of organized reading instruction, the emphasis has been on teaching the sounds of letters (Mathews 1966). It is instructive to consider why this should be the case, since there is no compelling evidence that formally teaching children phonics (the supposed "sounds" of letters) makes them readers, and no reason to believe that it could do so.

I have devoted long chapters in two books to outlining these arguments (Smith 1985, Ch. 4; 1994, Ch. 8). The "rules" of phonics are too complex (more than three hundred correspondences between letters and sounds) and too unreliable (there is no rule without exceptions—no letter that doesn't represent more than one sound, including silence, and no sound that can't be represented by more than one letter). The most flagrant exceptions to the rules occur in the most common words—such as *I, you, they, is, are, was, of, by, to, have, has,* and *mother*—much to the consternation of people who try to construct elementary reading materials out of words predictable through phonics.

It is no more possible to read by attempting to transform letters into comprehensible sounds than it is to spell by attempting to transform sounds into readable sequences of letters. The worst spellers are those who spell phonetically, just as the worst readers are those who try to sound out unfamiliar words according to the rules of phonics. Not even computers programmed with all the rules of phonics can convert written English to comprehensible sounds; they need to be programmed with the sounds of entire words (and the contexts in which those words can occur).

Nevertheless, reams of research claim to show that phonics should be the method of choice in teaching reading. The classic compilation is Chall (1967), whose title, *Learning to Read: The Great Debate*, I have echoed in this essay. A more recent volume is Adams (1990). The studies on which claims for the efficacy of phonics are based often compare children taught by one method with children taught by another method on criteria that fall far short of actual reading. Word identification rather than comprehension is the usual focus. Reading is seen as decoding to sound rather than the achievement of meaning, and there is almost always an underlying assumption that, one way or another, children must learn phonics.

So why does phonics instruction have such a seductive appeal, despite such conflicting or questionable research claims? Why do so many teachers feel that at least some phonics instruction is essential? The first reason must be that letters are such an obvious part of written language. Anyone who can read can recite (in a simplistic way) the correspondences of letters to sounds. Therefore, it is believed that teaching these correspondences will produce readers. The idea seems *manageable* from a methodological point of view. This is the same kind of reasoning that makes people believe that the way to teach computing, driving, or sailing is to teach the names of all the different parts and the mechanics of all the different functions.

A second explanation for the appeal of phonics is a fear that children won't learn if their learning isn't organized down to the smallest detail. Children can't be left to choose what and when they will learn—though they can make these choices perfectly well when learning to talk and to make sense of their world. It is a theory of innate wickedness, going back centuries, that if left to their own devices children will *resist* learning; they have to be *instructed* in a proper climate of authority and punishment. There has to be a *methodology* of teaching. Such reasoning has always been self-reinforcing. The fact that so many children have difficulty learning under systematic instructional discipline is taken as proof that they need still more systematic instructional discipline. Phonics and other structured methodologies have particular appeal to individuals who feel control is needed.

Of course, many children learn to read despite exposure to phonics. These children make phonics look good. In effect, phonics becomes a separate subject that they master. Phonics is always easy if you already know a word. Once you know that c-a-t spells "cat" you can say that "c" is pronounced \k\, and so forth. I know of no research on how many phonics rules children are capable of learning before they have begun to read, but it can't be many and they would certainly not be of much use. It is always the nonreaders who have trouble with phonics. And the blame is always put on these children for being "dyslexic" or for having other kinds of "specific learning disabilities" (all diagnosed by the fact that the children have failed to learn to read on the basis of phonics instruction). Or their teachers are blamed for not having tried hard enough or for failing to use the correct method.

Phonics also survives because there is no alternative method of teaching reading that is more successful. People who perceive learning from the official rather than the informal view don't consider that it might be methodology itself that fails. A change of method is no more significant for the learner than a change in the color of the walls in the classroom. But the failure of the alternative method is taken as a validation of phonics.

The Whole-Word Alternative

The traditional alternative to teaching reading through the sounds of letters has been the "whole-word" method of teaching complete words. In one sense, the whole word approach is unarguable. Children do learn to read by learning to recognize whole words. The more words they know, the easier it is to recognize and learn other words, based not on phonic correspondences but on syllabic and semantic resemblances. Whole words need to be recognized if they are to be pronounced correctly. Learning to read is basically a matter of learning to identify more and more written words, just as learning to talk is basically a matter of learning the meanings and uses of more and more spoken words. But the trouble with the whole-word method of teaching reading is that someone decides in advance the order in which the learner will be taught the individual words. This is about as useful to the beginning reader as it would be to tell children in advance the spoken words they are expected to learn in the course of each day. Words, spoken and written, are learned in meaningful contexts—at such times as the context is meaningful to the learner—not to suit the whims or theoretical predilections of an instructional designer.

The critics are right when they say that children can't learn to recognize enough whole words to become readers—not if they are expected to learn lists of words in advance of reading them. They must first become readers so that they can encounter new written words in meaningful contexts and in the company of supportive authors, just as they encounter new spoken words in the language of the company they keep. Children who can't learn and remember a dozen preselected words on a list after an hour of study can effortlessly learn and remember twenty words a day in interesting and meaningful contexts, where each new word is naturally made apparent to them, and naturally becomes part of them.

The "Whole Language" Alternative

Today the proponents of phonics have found a new enemy to take the place of the largely abandoned whole-word approach. The new enemy appears in a number of guises; it is usually called whole language (in North America and Australasia), real books (in Britain), and occasionally literature-based learning, language experience, or emergent literacy. It should be obvious that these alternatives are scarcely responsible for any recent decline in test scores; they have not been around long enough.

The majority of children are still confronted by some form of phonics instruction, aggravated by the growing harassment of discriminatory tests that add insult to injury.

However, the critics are once again half right. If regarded simply as another method of instruction, to be applied in another contrived environment, the whole language alternative and its variants may not succeed in teaching children to read. It is a travesty of the approach when confused teachers are required to adapt whole language instruction to traditional classroom structures and situations. And unfortunately large numbers of teachers regard whole language as just another method; they still don't trust children to learn unless their attention is controlled and their "progress" monitored and evaluated. They don't realize that the underlying principle is membership in the reading (and writing) club.

The original philosophy of whole language, even before it acquired the label, had nothing to do with methods, materials or techniques. There was no attempt to tell teachers what they should *do* to teach children to read; rather the aim was to tell teachers what their attitudes should be. The basis of the approach was *respect*—respect for language (which should be natural and "authentic," not contrived and fragmented), and respect for learners (who should be engaged in meaningful and productive activities, not in pointless drills and rote memorization). The philosophy has attracted the enthusiastic support of scores of thousands of teachers. It is without doubt the most vital movement in education today. Its political and social influence has been enormous (Willinski 1990).

But the whole language philosophy has also been exploited by many publishers, distorted by teachers who don't understand it, and misused by administrators incapable of modifying their organizational systems or theoretical mindsets. Administrators expect teachers to "apply" whole language without ensuring that the teachers understand what is involved or changing the circumstances in which they teach. There is no diminution of tests, and people are now devising oxymoronic whole language assessment instruments. Teachers who have no real idea of what they are doing say they are "doing whole language"—and again find reasons to blame children if they fail to learn.

There is the absurdity of teachers who offer children a narrow choice of books but provide no help in reading the one selected (which in any case is probably not a book the child would voluntarily choose if a wide selection were available). Children don't learn to read by osmosis (maliciously said to be a whole language belief), or by being left to their own devices. It may not be necessary to *instruct* children on how to read, but it is essential to encourage and assist them. Teachers don't abdicate responsibility when they embrace the philosophy of whole language (as they abdicate responsibility when they blindly work their way through a skills program). Instead, they accept the responsibility of ensuring that every child join the readers' club, fully admitted into the company of authors, not left frustrated at the threshold. It is the role of teachers, not of instructional methodologies, to teach.

The End of the Controversy?

Methods can never ensure that children learn to read. Children learn from people—from the teachers (formal and informal) who initiate them into the reading club and from the authors whose writing they read. It is the *relationships* that exist within the classroom that make the difference: the relationships that students have with their teachers and with each other, and their relationships with what they are supposed to be learning, with reading and writing. Tests are not required to find out whether they are learning; we need only observe what they are doing. If children are reading, with interest and without difficulty, they are learning to read (and learning other useful things as well).

Suppose I said that I met a child the other day, a seven-year-old, not doing too well in school, a little bored and apprehensive, possibly having trouble at home with an alcoholic parent or jealous of a new baby. Then suppose I asked you to tell me which specific aspect of reading this child should be studying and to name a book that would be guaranteed to hold this child's interest. You would rightly tell me that the task is absurd. No one could give a useful answer who could not even see the child. But while most people would be reluctant to answer such a question about a single individual, many have no hesitation in proposing the activities and books for an entire classroom of thirty individuals—and for every other child of the same age.

So when will the controversy end? When will phonics win the day, or be declared forever excluded from consideration? The realistic answer is probably never. The question is not one that research will resolve. Different kinds of research give different answers, depending on the theory of learning held by the researcher. Most teachers and administrators today are aware of the alternatives for teaching reading, but the position they adopt depends on the amount of power they are willing to relinquish.

People who don't trust children to learn—or teachers to teach—will always expect a method to do the job. Some enthusiasts of method actually believe that teachers are unnecessary, and that workbooks or computers will take care of learning. Many people vociferously protest that standards will collapse if a more humanistic approach is adopted, as if teaching children in circumstances that facilitate their learning, with less frustration and anguish all around, will somehow result in diminished abilities or lowered expectations.

There is also a belief that if there is no predetermined method then "anything goes" and teachers will not do their job responsibly. Regrettably, most teachers are taught to be dependent on methods and on the pronouncements of experts, so that inability to accept responsibility becomes a self-fulfilling prophesy.

Another common argument is that classrooms are too crowded for teachers to give every child individual attention. But teaching phonics requires giving every child individual attention, unless many are to be left by the wayside. The demands of a classroom in which everyone is enthusiastically and collaboratively reading and writing are much lighter on the teacher.

The objections continue, as they are bound to do in matters of such personal significance. (If teachers are to learn to behave differently, their own identities will be affected.) For example, the question is often asked, "What about children who can't learn in this way?"—usually an oblique reference to students from particular socioeconomic or ethnic groups, or diagnosed as having "learning problems." But if children from particular socioeconomic or ethnic groups do less well in school, then that is an indication of the bias of the school, not of the disabilities or "special needs" of the children. And if children experience difficulty in learning particular things at particular times—as most of them do at some time— then the answer is not that they need more application to methodologies (the systematic deprivation of experience) but that they must be shown more patience and sensitivity.

Not all children will learn what we want them to learn when we want them to learn it, no matter how understanding and collaborative their teachers might be. Children are individuals, no more to be standardized than adults can be standardized. The best we can do—and it is a great distance from where we are at the moment—is to do everything we can to promote interest and competence in literate activities and to ensure that there is a minimum of guilt and anguish on the part of teachers, students, or parents if not every child lives up to our hopes. Saying that we are determined to teach every child to read does not mean that we *will* teach every child to read. Nevertheless we could do much better than we are doing at the moment.

There is a strange idea that everything must be changed if anything is to change, that nothing can be improved unless everything is improved. Most teachers are good teachers some of the time and not so good, or downright awful, at other times. Good things happen in most schools some of the time, and regrettable things happen at other times.

The proportions need to be changed. The problem is that teachers, parents, and administrators often can't distinguish the desirable from the deplorable. There is a greater need for sensitivity than for new information, for willingness to explore than for determination to hold a position.

The great debate may never end. But perhaps it never should. The most productive way to deal with fundamental educational controversies might be to take them into every school and every community, to be dissected, discussed, and honestly argued. The endless debate over teaching reading could serve to keep teachers—and the public at large—conscious of the profound importance and delicacy of the noble art of teaching.

Chapter 5

Overselling Literacy

My concern is with the extravagent claims that are made for literacy and with the inflated manner in which literacy instruction and literacy research are frequently discussed. The ways in which reading and writing are often promoted, taught, and researched destroy the literacy that we are trying to create and discriminate against those whom literacy is supposed to liberate and enlighten. There are better ways to do what we're trying so hard to do.

Let me stress at the outset that I'm in favor of literacy. I think that people who don't read and write miss something in their lives. But I think the same about anyone who doesn't appreciate some form of music. Nevertheless, people who aren't musical aren't usually regarded as failures or social outcasts. They aren't blamed for poverty or unemployment. I don't see buttons or bumper stickers saying "Stamp Out Unmusicality," and I don't hear lack of musical ability referred to as a national disgrace. I don't think music would be helped much if war were declared on tone deafness.

Nobody makes extravagant promises about sensitivity to music, despite its benefits, but the same can't be said about literacy. Literacy is promoted as the source of just about everything that is good in this world, and illiteracy is cited as the cause of widespread evil. I'm concerned about the way this is done—and with the consequences.

Overselling Literacy

Literacy is talked of as the "golden key" to everything from full employment and a reduced crime rate to the treasures of world literature and culture. I know, I've talked that way myself. But is it true? Literacy doesn't make anyone a better person. Some of the greatest tyrants have been voracious readers and compelling writers. Some people believe that making all young people literate would prevent crime, but I don't think that inability to read and write makes anyone a criminal— something else is going on. And I haven't seen any evidence that learning to read makes criminals abandon their nefarious practices. If anything it would make them more efficient criminals.

Literacy doesn't generate finer feelings or higher values. It doesn't even make anyone smarter. Illiterate people navigated the oceans by reading the stars, which for millennia served many cultures as clock, calendar, atlas, almanac, and historical record. Today, most literate people don't even notice the stars. People who can't read and write think just as well out of school as people who can read and write (Scribner and Cole 1978), especially if they are members of a culture in which strong oral-language traditions have prevailed (Scollon and Scollon 1981). Even people who used to claim that reading and writing make us think and talk differently (Olson 1977) have changed their minds (Olson 1987). They now acknowledge that any change in language or thought is a consequence of living in a literate society, where the existence of print is likely to make everyone think and talk differently, whether or not they can read and write.

What they read and write may make people smarter—but so will any activity that engages the mind, including interesting conversation. And children in school are rarely taught what *is* worthwhile reading and writing. Instead, reading and writing are used for school chores.

Literacy doesn't guarantee anyone a job; this is a tragic deception too often perpetrated on the young. Many unemployed people are literate, and many people with jobs are scarcely literate. Literacy doesn't create employment. When an unemployed person gets a job, it is usually at the expense of someone else from the same community who becomes or remains unemployed. The world is not crying out for more literate people to take on jobs, but for more job opportunities for the literate and unlettered alike.

Literacy doesn't guarantee work, any more than learning to drive guarantees that you'll get a car. But just as giving everyone a car would soon result in most people learning to drive, so work almost guarantees literacy, at least the job-related kind of literacy that we strive so mightily and unsuccessfully to develop in the schools. Mechanics quickly learn to read their manuals and to write their estimates, short-order cooks learn to read orders, and servers learn to write them, even if they would fail standardized reading tests. Most people read more on the job than they ever did in school (Mikulecky 1982). Despite the mythology, there are few people who can't read traffic signs and product names.

Many children can do the kind of reading I am talking about—the reading that is important in a familiar environment—before they come to school. Learning on the job to do job-related reading and writing is no mean accomplishment—indeed, it is all that many professional people are able to do. People in lower-paid jobs may not be able to read what the professionals read, but the professionals probably can't read the specialized materials of other occupations. Doctors, lawyers, and teachers may not read (or not be able to read) the novels and magazines that mechanics and short-order cooks read.

Learning the "basic skills" of reading and writing doesn't make anyone literate—not if by *literate* we mean able to make use of the possibilities of written language. The professionals who never read or write anything beyond work-related material should perhaps not be called literate; if they're not working they don't read and write. But by such a severe criterion, how many teachers are literate? Many students leave school having learned the "basics" of reading and writing but with no inclination ever to pursue these activities voluntarily; they have no understanding of what literacy can do for them apart from getting them through school. How literate are they? Literacy is not a set of skills or a finished state; it is an attitude toward the world. A literate attitude makes learning to read and write possible and productive.

The "War" on Illiterates

When literacy is promoted as the cure for all economic, social, and educational problems, it is easy to assume that inability to read and write *causes* economic, social, and educational ills. Literacy becomes a caste mark, and those who haven't got it are discriminated against. They are blamed for our troubles. Inability to read and write comes to be regarded as a disease that must be "treated" or "cured." It is an epidemic that must be "eradicated," an enemy that must be "wiped out." "War" is declared on illiteracy, and "campaigns" are organized to "attack" it.

The December 1987 issue of *Reading Today* reported that a senior official of the International Reading Association (IRA) told a Senate Subcommittee on Education in August 1987 that the United States would never "solve the problem" of adult illiteracy without a national policy on literacy. The same journal issue reported that the American Newspaper

Publishers' Association had renewed efforts to "fight illiteracy" with a three-year "assault on illiteracy." Together the IRA and ANPA unveiled a poster they described as "perfect for classrooms, school offices, and homes." It depicted dinosaurs and asserted, "READ, avoid extinction." No wonder people who are identified (or who identify themselves) as illiterate may have a problem.

Money spent on literacy programs may be diverted from more workable programs focussed on poverty and unemployment. If well-housed, well-fed, well-clothed, and employed people tend to read better than others, perhaps it would be more effective to attend to the welfare of poor readers rather than to their accomplishments in literacy.

Having been misconstrued as a cause of social problems, illiteracy is then used as a weapon. Students who don't read and write don't fit into the educational system, therefore students who don't appear likely to fit into the system aren't expected to be readers and writers. They aren't treated as prospective readers and writers (Shannon 1985). The students who don't fit into the system see themselves as actual or potential illiterates, and everyone's prophesy is fulfilled. Students who are expected to have difficulty with reading and writing are considered outcasts, lose self-respect, and are persuaded that they *can't be* readers and writers—even as we claim to be teaching them literacy. The language that is used to describe people who don't read and write well can be reminiscent of some of the most prejudiced ways in which handicapped people, or racial and other minorities, are talked about. Giroux (1983) has proposed that "poor students" are an oppressed minority who "act out" the way they are perceived as a form of resistance.

Overselling Instruction

I shall not devote a lot of space to this issue because I have discussed it extensively elsewhere, notably in *Insult to Intelligence* (Smith 1986), in which I argue that the bureaucratic control of classrooms through prescribed instruction and standardized tests is an affront to the intelligence of students and teachers alike. The subject is depressing, not least because the situation doesn't seem to be getting any better.

But I must emphasize the continuing hyperbole behind it all. Over 500 publishers and other exhibitors participate in IRA conventions, most of them blithely claiming that their materials and tests would succeed in teaching children to read or solve "learning problems." They don't acknowledge that the personal relationship between a student and a teacher might determine whether a student learns to read; that materials and techniques can never be trusted. The history of prepackaged instructional programs, whether produced commercially or in federally funded laboratories, has been one of total *failure*.

The only rationale for the new materials and approaches that are introduced every year must be the inadequacy of everything produced previously. Yet none of the instructional developers specify *how* they have managed to discover the key that has eluded themselves and everyone else in the past. They simply assume—and loudly proclaim— that the new method will work. The fact that the biggest commercial programs are routinely updated every year or two should alert us to the inevitability that today's programs are destined to be found obsolete and inadequate tomorrow.

The exhibitors' announcements at a recent IRA convention were typically grandiloquent. For example, Harcourt Brace Jovanovich heralded "an invitation to a lifetime of reading" with a "totally new" K–8 program that "develops both the ability and desire to read," and a spelling program that "will help every student move ahead." Merrill's "Spelling for Word Mastery" program (grades 1–8) offered "preorganized teaching material" to help teachers and students perform at their very best every day. Riverside Publishing Co. exploited the convention theme of "Reaching new heights in literacy" to claim that their programs and tests put new heights within the grasp of teachers, while Macmillan simply presented their name and materials against a backdrop of Mount Everest (the convention slogan did the rest for them). Open Court claimed that its *Headway Basal Reading* series would give *all* students the foundation of strategies they need to know *how* to get the right answers (copywriter's emphasis), and Scott, Foresman announced new "integrated" programs that would teach reading and writing "and still have time for aerobics." It would be too easy and too tedious to continue. It is all just advertising hype, of course, but it obviously works; it is the basis on which instructional programs are purchased and classroom practices determined. And now all the reading and writing programs are going onto computers, with even more outrageous claims about the success that will be achieved, often without the involvement or interference of teachers.

All of these programs ignore the fact that literacy is a social phenomenon. Individuals don't become literate from the formal instruction they receive, but from what they read and write about, and the people they read and write with. Learning is also a social phenomenon. What everyone in every culture has taken for granted for millennia (until experimental psychologists took the study of learning out of the real world and put it in the laboratory) is that learning is a simple consequence of the company you keep. Children accepted into a community of music lovers learn about music; those who join a group of hockey players learn to play hockey; those who affiliate with gangs learn to do what gangs do. Deliberate efforts to instruct are not required, indeed they typically fail, especially if accompanied by fulsome praise for the abstract value of what is to be learned. Learning is produced by mutual participation in interesting activities, not by panegyrics.

Objectives and Evaluation

Behind all the instructional programs, all the classroom materials and techniques, is the notion that learning can be improved, if not guaranteed, when what is to be learned is spelled out one little bit at a time, in the form of *objectives* that the learner must attain. Each objective must be mastered before moving on to the next. The idea is that ability develops out of the systematic acquisition of skills and bits of information (learn first and do later), rather than as a consequence of facilitated engagement in meaningful activities (do now, and learn incidentally). However, there is absolutely no evidence that the specification of objectives or rigidly constructed teacher manuals and curriculum guides facilitate learning, despite more than thirty years of concentrated effort. On the contrary, programmatic instruction can only be regarded as the systematic deprivation of experience. Yet so highly touted has "objective," externally controlled instruction become that some people can't imagine any alternative. The more we expect or claim a method of teaching literacy to be foolproof, the more we are going to blame teachers and students for failure. The situation is not unfamiliar. All authoritarian regimes claim the credit when things go well, and hold their victims responsible for shortcomings.

The IRA official I mentioned earlier told the Senate Subcommittee that "solving the illiteracy problem" would require coordination of existing federal, state, local, and private programs; collecting information; linking training to the needs of the state and the community; and research on the levels of literacy needed for a variety of occupations. How more bureaucratic organization and even more demographic data were supposed to help individuals become members of a literate community was not specified; the power of centralized management of teaching practices was taken for granted.

All of which leads to the miserable topic of evaluation. This is not the place to expound upon the enormous damage done by the mania for testing and measurement, by distracting and discouraging teachers and students alike. All over the continent, teachers are busy preparing students (or learning to prepare students) to take mandated reading and writing tests, when they might otherwise be helping the students to engage in worthwhile literacy. Students never learn anything constructive about reading and writing by being told what poor students they are, and teachers never become better teachers by being harassed about the extent of the task ahead of them.

I simply want to refer to the gross overselling of evaluation, to the incredible notion that students will learn more (and teachers will teach better) if there is continual detailed monitoring of everything the student is supposed to learn. I have never seen evidence that testing produces literacy, though there are massive indications that it has the opposite effect. Yet "evaluation" always tops the list when anyone wants to improve educational practice. Any proposal that does not include "evaluation" would be regarded as inadequate and incompetent.

I don't know what happened to common sense (let alone expertise) as a way of judging the soundness of a proposal or the relevance of a classroom practice, but it is clear that the "objective" alternative of counting and comparing units of learning is simply a bureaucratic myth. Evaluation is grossly overrated—it is time that the perfidious practice itself was subjected to some critical evaluation.

Overselling Research

The IRA's Annual Review of Reading Research currently publishes summaries of over 1000 research reports every year, all of them related in one way or another to literacy or literacy instruction. More than 80 percent of these studies, according to Barr (1986), are experimental; most of the rest relate to investigations within classrooms. Scarcely any of these studies look at how children become literate in circumstances that are not artificially manipulated.

These days it seems to be expected that research will solve all our problems for us. If there is anything we can't make up our minds about, we expect research to do it for us. Actually I should have said that research is expected to make up other people's minds, because it is rare to find anyone whose own point of view has been changed by research. Research is capable of producing any evidence or answer that we want; it can support any preconception.

Research is never atheoretical, and experimenters get what they look for. What is technically referred to as "controlling extraneous variables" means ignoring factors the researcher isn't interested in. One can never get beyond the preconceptions of the researcher in relating educational research to practice. IRA convention programs are full of research reports advancing contradictory points of view, promoting or rejecting phonics instruction, recommending or condemning basal readers, urging or deriding direct instruction. *Some* researchers (at least) must be wrong.

If all the educational research ever done were to be regarded as one huge experiment, the only conclusion that could be drawn would be overwhelming support for the null hypothesis that educational research has made no significant difference to literacy. (And I would argue that the same conclusions can be drawn from all the recent work in neurophysiology.) Most teaching is still done in the same old ways with the same old degree of success; only the excuses have changed. "New knowledge" is proclaimed to justify old prejudices. And we may be entering an even more narrow-minded era as "cognitive scientists" refuse to entertain theories about learning or comprehension that can't be simulated by computers.

Only one kind of research has had anything useful to say about literacy, and that is *ethnographic* or *naturalistic* research—studies observing how literacy is actually learned and used in real communities, without the researchers' trying to manipulate the situation in any way. Not surprisingly, such studies have uniformly shown that literacy and learning are sociocultural phenomena (here, too, the research reflects the perspective of the researchers). However, the usual encomiums have been conspicuously lacking for ethnographic research, largely I suspect because it offers nothing to the bureaucrat, administrator, or publisher who can't profit from the evidence that literacy flourishes with a relaxation of external pressure and control.

One conclusion, however, must be drawn from such studies of states of affairs in the real world. It is the reassuring and revolutionary implication that children and adults can and frequently do learn to read and write, do become literate, not as a result of instructional programs, or evaluation, or research, or indeed of fulsome claims about the importance of literacy, but simply through association with literate people.

Children don't learn from what we exhort them to do, but from what they see us doing. They aren't going to learn from our telling them that literacy will help them achieve excellence, or unlock the doors to treasures of world literature, or scale new heights. Thinking about our propensity for telling other people what is good for them reminds me that the International Reading Association must be the largest voluntary organization in the world dedicated to the proposition that it is good for other people to do something. It is not necessary to be a practicing reader to belong to the IRA, any more than it is necessary to be a practicing reader to teach reading. Both are predicated on the belief that other people should be readers.

Children learn from what they see us doing—that is what ethnographic research demonstrates. And usually they learn that reading and writing are boring, painful, and useless activities. Wherever do they get such ideas?

What Good Is Literacy?

The things that literacy is good for have to be demonstrated personally; they are not compelling if simply talked about. As Eliza Doolittle complained to Professor Higgins on a somewhat different topic, "Don't talk of love, *show me.*"

The enjoyment of stories is a good example. Children can't learn to read merely with the promise that literacy will bring the delights of something called stories. Children must know what stories are, and be shown that reading provides access to them. In other words, until they can read stories for themselves, other people must read stories to them and with them. But first, children must see other people reading stories for their own pleasure. All this should seem elementary enough, but many children don't get the opportunity to be read to, at home or at school, and they are often expected to learn to read (as a meaningless activity) before they get a chance to discover stories. Most students *never* see their teachers reading for their own pleasure. What they see is what they learn, that reading is a variety of rituals, frequently meaningless and sometimes punitive, engaged in reluctantly by teachers and students. Still fewer students see teachers writing anything that is not a routine classroom chore, and few students have the opportunity to experience personally the achievement and satisfaction that writing can bring.

But the pleasures and satisfaction of literacy are more than stories. Reading and writing help the brain achieve what the brain does best— the creation of worlds. Imagination is the essence of mental life, the foundation of comprehension, learning, remembering, and reasoning, in public and in private. Reading and writing provide opportunities for the imagination to be exercised in manners and to extents in no other way possible. Literacy offers these advantages to individuals in all cultures, at all socioeconomic levels, to the employed and the unemployed alike.

But children—and unlettered adults—can learn none of this from extravagant recommendations or national campaigns. Telling students what they lose if they don't become practicing readers and writers can only serve to frustrate them; they have to be *shown*. It is the easiest thing in the world for parents and teachers to help students to read and to write—until authors can take over as the real teachers of literacy (Meek 1988). The demonstrations and collaboration not only provide a motive for learning, they take care of the learning.

There is a second good reason to learn to become readers and writers; literacy can be *powerful*. It can do more than transform thought, it can transform the world. Literacy can raise social consciousness and provide a means for the expression and fulfilment of this consciousness. But once again, there is no way this can be understood through alluring descriptions and unwarranted guarantees; it has to be experienced. Paulo Freire's pedagogic technique raises social consciousness not as a way of using literacy but as a means of acquiring it (Freire 1972, 1982). Children have to see that literacy is power—the way they see that money is power—by observing the powerful ways other people use it.

How often do students get the opportunity to see literacy being used in powerful ways in school? Power can be exercised only by autonomous individuals, and the degree of power that many teachers have to transform their own social reality, and that of their students, is limited indeed. Their efforts to achieve such authority could provide teachers with the best means to present literacy to students who have reading and writing "problems."

The Alternative

I am by no means sure that universal literacy can be attained. Too much is wrong with the way our schools and society are organized. But if literacy is to flourish it will be in schools and if literacy dies it will also be in schools. So I would like to see schools become more literate places.

We should talk less about the importance of literacy, and stop talking altogether about achieving it through better objectives and management. Talking about achieving literacy leads to the same tired old language: the "problem" will be solved with new programs, more extensive evaluation, and better objectives. But we have had all these nostrums before and must at last acknowledge that they have failed.

The alternative is to ask what *kind* of schools we want. We know the social conditions under which learning and literacy almost inevitably occur; those environments must be established in schools. It comes down to a question of personal relationships.

What kind of relationship do we want students to have with each other—competitive (because not everyone is going to get high grades) or cooperative (because we stop organizing students according to age and ability)? What kind of relationship do we want teachers to have with each other—isolationist and territorial (because teachers are rarely welcome in one another's classrooms) or collaborative (because they help each other to engage in authentic activities with their students)? And what kind of relationship do we want teachers and students to have—antagonistic (because anyone who administers the tests and distributes the grades must be an adversary) or collegial (because everyone engages in patently interesting and worthwhile activities)?

Of course, there is no way that students will be empowered until teachers themselves are empowered, and this will not happen until teachers are autonomous in their classrooms. Teachers can be held accountable by their peers and by the community in which they work, but not told by external authorities precisely how they should teach.

The basic issue is political: who will be in charge of classrooms—teachers or outsiders? All the prescribed programs, all the pre-specified and detailed objectives, and all the mandated assessments are impositions from outside. They interfere not only with the autonomy of teachers but with the ability of teachers and students to act together in pursuit of learning. Two other factors cloud the issue. The first is the way in which teachers themselves are taught, the "teacher training" which strips many young teachers in advance of any autonomy they might have, conditioning them to depend on "experts" and on prepackaged programs and tests, rather than on experience, independent judgment, and the personal knowledge that only they can have of the students for whom they are responsible. The second confounding factor—which has been the subject of this essay—is all the hyperbole about literacy, and also about instruction, evaluation, and research, which misleads and discriminates.

I see but one solution for all these problems. Teachers must become more professional; they must regain control of classrooms, assert themselves politically, and demand that all outside interference in educational practice be halted. It is right that society should expect teachers to teach particular things. But no one should prescribe and pace the ways in which that teaching should be done.

How are teachers to achieve this autonomy? The issue centers on the professional and political status of teachers, and demands their professional and political response. No bureaucratic decision about teaching or evaluation should escape public examination. No intrusion into how teachers should teach should go unchallenged. Teachers should use the media in the ways the media are used against them, not just with press releases but with participation in public affairs broadcasts, debates, letters to editors, and feature-page articles. But first, teachers must themselves become fully sensitive to what is going on. Their own consciousness of the reality of contemporary education must be raised if they are to raise the consciousness of society.

I have said that literacy is good for two things—the pursuit of the individual imagination and the exercise of personal power. Teachers can demonstrate the first by focussing on reading and writing that jointly interest them and their students. Teachers need not wait for the interest to appear; they can *promote* interest by demonstrating their own interests. Nothing attracts young people more than activities, abilities, or secrets that absorb adults; they want to know about the things we find worthwhile. Demonstrating and collaborating in the imaginative possibilities of literacy should be a classroom delight for teachers and students alike.

But it is in the efforts of teachers to apprehend the reality of their own condition that the *power* of literacy can be demonstrated. Teachers must understand which classroom practices are worthwhile (because they foster interest, collaboration, confidence, and learning) and which are detrimental (because they generate only boredom, disinterest, discouragement, competition, and discrimination).

Every aspect of the classroom day must be analyzed, not only for its content and the attention it demands, but for its historical and theoretical justification and for its effects on teachers and students. Such a persistent reflective inquiry demands that teachers and students work together to gain a conceptual command of the world they jointly inhabit, and that they engage in a constant literate endeavor to master the origins and consequences of their condition. When students of any age see teachers striving to understand and control the situation in their own classrooms, through reading, writing, reflection, discussion, and action, then the power of literacy will indeed be revealed and developed. Only teachers *and* students together can gain the authority to recapture control of education in the schools, and only teachers *as* students can acquire and exercise the power to liberate education at teacher-training institutions. Change must come from the roots.

From another point of view, I am talking about thinking in action. The latest and culminating absurdity in the external control of education is the notion that critical thinking itself can be promoted by new curriculum objectives, more prepackaged instruction, and of course, more tests. If anything, thinking has been destroyed in classrooms by the very methods now proposed to promote it. Students are supposed to learn to think through exercises that demonstrate that teachers themselves are not expected to be creative and critical thinkers. Teachers of reading and writing could begin to take charge by resisting the movement to "teach" thinking. They have been there before. They have seen what the hyperbole, the outside control of instruction and evaluation, and the inflated claims of "research" have done for literacy. It is not necessary for education to go through the long, wasteful, and destructive process again with respect to thought.

The literate inquiry and action needed to transform education can themselves demonstrate and encourage literacy and thinking in the classroom. And that is no overstatement.

Chapter 6

What Good Is a Teacher in the Information Age?

Teachers are in danger of becoming an endangered species. They are criticized, disparaged, accused of dereliction of duty, and blamed for declining standards. At the same time, their resources are reduced and they are frequently told exactly what, when, and how they should teach. They are trapped between inflated expectations and diminished autonomy, directed to teach flexibly, sensitively, and creatively, yet denied the authority to do so. They are often required to follow mechanically the guidelines and timetables established by distant committees, and threatened with replacement by machines if they are not more successful.

Social, economic, and technological developments bring new attitudes toward education, many of them not propitious for teachers. Their extinction is a distinct possibility. The technology to replace classroom teachers already exists—and so do people who think that teachers are expensive anachronisms. If teachers are not careful, they could become as obsolete as ostlers.

Nevertheless, most teachers, supported by a few parents and others outside the profession, regard themselves as the essential keystone of education, more important than technology, plant, materials, tests, guidelines, administrators, professors, and politicians put together, perfectly able to perform their role without any of these adjuncts and appendages, in fact often better without them.

I believe that the importance of teachers lies in the very fact that they are not machines, which they should not try to emulate. The current images of what teachers should be and how they should behave are fallacious, and so is the belief that teachers can be improved and even replaced by technology.

What good is a teacher? I propose first to look at a conventional expectation of how teachers should teach, and admit that many teachers are not much good at teaching in this way. But I argue that the conventional view does not define the primary role of teachers. The conventional view is misguided.

I then consider the technology that is beginning to infiltrate education, the technology of the Internet, the "information highway." This technology is a threat to teachers precisely because it can conform so closely to conventional belief about the nature of education and teaching.

I go on to describe what I see as the true role of teachers, and to discuss why technology should not be permitted to usurp this role (though teachers should not be afraid to take control of technology). I am not saying that all teachers are exemplary. This could hardly be expected considering the pressures upon them. But I shall outline my view of what teachers are good for. At this point I can express in just six words the natural, primary, and inescapable function of teachers that cannot be handed over to any kind of technology: it is *to provide examples and make choices*. In one word, the role of teachers is to be *influential*, which today is precisely what they are not.

Finally, I shall briefly consider how teachers might become influential, and preserve themselves and their role—given much more action on their part and the support of allies that they themselves must recruit. Teachers can't expect other people to rescue them; they must save themselves.

What Teachers Are For—
The Conventional View

At its very simplest—which is the way the belief is usually held and expressed—the conventional view is that the job of teachers is to get *information* into students in systematic and orderly ways. (The key word used to be "knowledge," but it was superseded when we entered the "information age" and has just about disappeared now that the information highway has arrived. The word *facts*, which is what information is generally seen as being, is itself losing ground to "data" and to even more arcane terms like "parameters." The new terms tend to be adopted eagerly and used unreflectively, their clarity and relevance being taken for granted.) Sometimes teachers are expected to provide information for their students themselves, but usually their role is perceived as transmitting information through books, worksheets, movies, videos, and the monitors of computer terminals.

The "information" view applies from kindergarten to graduate school. Teachers may be told precisely what information they should "teach" by edicts or guidelines from bureaucratic authorities or by patterns laid down in textbooks or in the pathways of computer software.

Students and teachers are expected to be kept on track on the "learning task" through constant monitoring, reflected in the contemporary obsession with tests, including the insidious practice of publishing league tables of school and classroom "achievement." The bromide term "excellence," when it means anything at all, refers to performance on these tests.

The conventional view regards learning as *memorization*, with students ready to "move ahead" once tests of recall are passed. When learning is not demonstrated, the standard procedure includes correction, exhortations to work harder, further practice, public shaming, and eventual "withdrawal" into groups receiving more correction, more drill, lower expectations of achievement, and social stigmatization.

Teachers are also expected to teach *skills*. This vague term is often applied to activities requiring physical dexterity and coordination (like handwriting, "keyboarding," dance, and sports), but also to behaviors primarily involving knowledge rather than deftness (such as "library skills" and "computer skills"), and even to broad categories that depend almost entirely on experience—such as reading, writing, and spelling. Any difference there might be between skills and information learning becomes irrelevant when the method of teaching is rooted in repetition and reinforcement. The role of the teacher is always to see that students stay on task and try harder.

The conventional view of learning has a long history, broadly based on efforts to make teaching "scientific." Major influences were the technology of the production line, the manipulative methodology of laboratory experimentation, systems analysis, program planning and evaluation, quality control, rigorous accountancy and accountability, and other sources as diverse as intensive animal-rearing practices and military tactics (Smith 1986).

Almost all major political developments in education in the last hundred years have been based on the conventional view of learning, promoted by industrial or engineering technicians, behavioristically inclined scientists, and efficiency-oriented bureaucrats, rather than on the perceptions of philosophers, anthropologists, writers, artists, and even experienced classroom teachers. Changes almost inevitably rely on the assumption that teaching and learning depend on control, and that the way to improve education is to increase control, of both teachers and students.

The conventional view bears no resemblance to the way anyone actually learns, in school or out, though many administrators, parents, and even teachers believe it reflects their own education. The conventional view is a distorting lens through which they recall and rationalize their own experience. In fact, rote memorization through repetition and testing is the least effective way to learn or to teach. Not surprisingly, teachers find the objective-based "information" approach frustrating, tedious, and time-consuming, although some welcome the way it releases them from responsibility for making decisions in the classroom. Most try to leaven the experience for themselves and their students by introducing personal, spontaneous, and interesting interludes.

The conventional view leaves little room for individual differences among teachers or students, personal idiosyncrasies, values, attitudes, variations in past experience, and even interest and desire. Since these human characteristics are not amenable to scientific or bureaucratic control, they are regarded as "unscientific" or irrelevant. The wretched endeavor to make intrinsically boring material and activities interesting has resulted in efforts to make all learning "entertaining" and "fun." There is even a new word for this flourishing enterprise in the communications industry—*edutainment*.

Values are taught (if certified to be politically correct) as content. So are citizenship, politics, entrepreneurism, consumerism, and interpersonal relations. The criterion of learning is not demeanor but the ability to answer questions. "Standards" are scores on tests, not modes of behavior. Motivation is demanded, although enthusiasm is not expected and can't be handled. Learning is regarded as "work" and students who fail to learn are considered to be either handicapped or lazy. Students are sometimes expected to "take charge" of their own learning. This does not mean that they pursue their own interests, but that they commit themselves to achieve ends established for them and their teachers by remote authorities.

Teachers are required to learn "teaching skills." Their training (note the word) is methodology-driven rather than experience-based. On the assumption that teachers can't be trusted to make educational decisions, they are given no opportunity to do so. Many teachers learn to be passive, seeing their role as intermediaries rather than as initiators.

Teachers in general are not good at teaching in mechanical information-transmission ways—machines are better. But before I outline what teachers *are* good for, that no technology can offer, I must discuss a pervasive contemporary technology that conforms almost perfectly to the conventional view of teaching. It is being promoted, by its own producers and by others, as the ideal means of bringing information to students, thereby ensuring learning.

The Technology at the Door

There has already been one major attempt, in the 1980s, to replace teachers with electronic technology, using desktop computers or local terminals as "teaching machines" (or "learning machines"—the terms were used indiscriminately). Many examples of "drill and test" hardware and software still exist, most of it fortunately little used. The basic idea was that computers could deliver repetitive instruction in more insistent and entertaining ways than human teachers, while simultaneously monitoring, testing, and record keeping. The program designers saw themselves as teachers, more cost-effective than anyone actually in the classroom because there were many fewer of them and they were "experts" (Smith 1986). The attempt was crude and premature. It harnessed learners to preset procedures, and the only interactivity it offered was limited branching on prefabricated loops. Students could not question the instruction, make extended responses, pursue interesting digressions, or move independently in new directions, either by themselves or with the aid of a classroom teacher.

None of these deficiencies is a concern today. All of the technical problems have been solved by the simple but gargantuan expedient of linking computers together through the telephone system, first into "local area networks" that pool resources and bring neighboring operators into direct contact, and then by linking individual networks into one great globe-spanning system of essentially infinite depth and complexity. Now learners can reach any teacher or teaching material in the world—and any teacher or teaching material in the world can reach learners. The "information highway" has arrived. The Internet is referred to as a system, but it was largely unplanned and even unexpected, evolving spontaneously from the small-scale independent activities of many individuals rather than at their behest or on their behalf. It is neither systematic nor predictable, more of an all-pervasive and constantly developing environment or climate. The world has never seen anything like it before, and we do not have an apt word with which to categorize it (any more than we have an apt term to characterize the kind of machine a computer is).

Rather than speculate on the largely unimaginable future effects of the technology on education, and on life in general, I offer a brief sketch of what the technology is already able to do. The system functions with familiar devices that exist in most homes, offices, and institutions (including schools), and that are likely to be "upgraded" in the normal course of events, especially when many people seem unable to resist the allure of electronic gadgetry for themselves or for others. Those devices are the telephone, television, and the personal computer.

Some current possibilities of computer networks are well known, such as electronic mail, bulletin boards, conferences and interviews, and access to dictionaries, directories, encyclopedias, professional and scientific manuals and resources, library indexes, entertainment guides, shopping catalogs, airline timetables, weather forecasts, real estate listings, culinary demonstrations, sports, and movies.

Inquiry on the information highway is not the same as looking up a book in a library; it is "interactive." On Internet you can eavesdrop on conversations and participate in clubs and special interest groups, asking questions and receiving answers. You can discover pathways into new and even unexpected areas. You can command "information" that will be sent to you almost instantaneously—and you will also be sent information that you did not request, anticipate, and possibly do not want. A complementary side of the interaction not so often heard about is that other people have access to you, whether you want it or not.

Other people can also obtain information from you, regarding your family, financial, medical and educational history, your purchasing habits, political affiliations, personal beliefs, and credit card numbers. If you are like most people, you will disclose much of this information trustingly. If you don't, it can easily be obtained from other sources. You can conduct much of your correspondence, purchasing, banking, education, and other affairs on the system; you can vote and participate in political activities on it, and soon there may be no other way of doing many of those things except through the two-way thoroughfares of the information highway.

As I write these words there are at least 50,000 computer networks in 135 countries around the world, with over 20,000,000 users able to communicate with each other and to make use of more than 3,000,000 free programs and information sources. I am reluctant to cite these statistics because they will be hopelessly outdated by the time they are published, let alone read. There are nets within nets and nets over nets. "Database publishers" are making multi-billion-dollar deals and mergers, investing in "information" which they confidently expect to market on a massive scale. Many of them used to publish books, periodicals, or newspapers, and may still do so as a decreasing proportion of their activities. Telephone companies are renewing their equipment for multimedia integration—so that telephones, television sets, and computers in every home and office (and educational institution) will act as one compact component of a worldwide system. Giant computer hardware and software manufacturers produce material "dedicated" to education. Publishers are now putting their products "on line" so that libraries and educational institutions as well as government and commercial concerns can save money and improve coverage by purchasing information and literature in electronic rather than paper form. Anyone nostalgic enough to prefer paper can print out a personal copy of exactly what is desired, no more and no less. This is not the place to dwell on the cataclysmic effect all this will have on authors.

Material on the information highway can be tagged for specific "newsgroups," targeted to selected users (which could be as small as just one person), all connected by "usenets." If you want to aim a product or a message (or an exercise) to all left-handed, blue-eyed bilingual fourteen-year-old females—no problem. Don't object that some possibilities are just too absurd, or that others will be overlooked—anything that anyone wants will become possible. Every objection will be taken care of. Electronic "servers" (information distributors) *welcome* being shown deficiencies in the system, so they can rush to fill profitable gaps.

Libraries are already choosing electronic data over books and journals, driven by budgets as well as by supplier pressure and consumer demand, and the trend is just beginning. A reaction in favor of books is no more likely than a movement to abandon automobiles in favor of horse transport. Computer network education, in-house and "distance learning," is already well established, with growing numbers of students getting undergraduate and advanced degrees and other diplomas without ever meeting a teacher face-to-face. "Electronic learning" is not a trend that will be reversed, in fact it is beginning to be manifested in high schools, in commercial "tutorial" enterprises, and in home schooling. It claims to be much more effective and interesting than "old-fashioned" teaching and learning.

Electronic technology is a threat to teachers precisely because it conforms so closely to conventional beliefs about the nature of education, learning, and teaching. How long before teachers become roadkill on the information highway?

You may object that someone must keep an eye on students, to ensure that they stay in school and on task. But you should be careful in suggesting that teachers perform a primarily custodial or child-sitting function. Cheaper means will be found for these purposes than teachers and school buildings.

You may object that there would be no need for schools with electronic education. You'd be right. Most homes have most of the necessary equipment already, and it would be cheaper to install the rest than to keep building and maintaining schools. It would also conform to the tenor of the times in deinstitutionalizing communal services. Growing numbers of people are expected to work at home, felons are sentenced to confinement at home, and many patients are assured they can receive better care at home than in the hospital.

It is not difficult to imagine the information highway driving straight through schools, making many teachers unnecessary. Everything that is needed is in place already, or could be provided relatively inexpensively with funds shifted from other parts of the educational budget, like library books, text books, teacher salaries, buildings, and maintenance. Decisions about the timetabling and content of student activity on the network could be made centrally, at district levels or beyond. In fact, the possibility of central control, and monitoring of results, would be one of the attractions of the system. No need to fear that instruction will not be "individualized"—every student, like every other consumer of every other product, could be reached directly and immediately, according to whatever criteria anyone decides should be relevant.

The tide of information technology is already seeping under the doors of our classrooms and could inundate education with startling suddenness. People in the information industry—from global corporations to individual entrepreneurs—are straining to exploit the vast market of education through political power and alluring advertising. They appeal to everyone who believes that learning is synonymous with the acquisition of information. And there are people in education—administrators, accountants, and politicians, but also many parents—who will find the combination of budgetary reductions and "improved" efficiency irresistible. It would be ingenuous to expect a few dissident teachers (or a mass of apathetic ones) to hold off the flood.

What Is a Teacher?

What is the contrast? The alternative point of view is that learning is as natural as physical growth, in fact it *is* growth, the development of the individual, grounded in identification and involvement, nurtured by experience, and patterned by the company we keep. We learn to be like the people we see ourselves as being like, from the company we keep. I have elaborated on this point of view elsewhere in this book and in other publications (Smith 1988, 1990).

In a general sense, teachers are the people who show us, knowingly or not, how things are done, and who assist us, knowingly or not, to do them ourselves. In effect, they protect learners. Learning is a communal activity. We learn to do the things we see people around us doing, if we want to do those things ourselves, and we come to know the things they know, usually quite unconsciously.

Young people often have difficulty learning what adults would like them to learn, but that is because they do not see themselves doing those things. Young people usually have no problem learning adult habits, even (and perhaps especially) when adults would prefer them not to do so. Adults become unwitting teachers, doing precisely what any teacher has to do to ensure learning—demonstrating that an activity is satisfying and attainable.

Deliberately setting someone up as a model for other people to copy rarely succeeds. Instead we all unconsciously *follow examples*—the examples of things we would like to do ourselves, which we see ourselves doing.

The overriding advantage and necessity of professional teachers lies in the fact that they are *people* with whom learners can identify and collaborate. They constitute exemplars themselves, and they provide access to other people who can be identified with, to members of the communities and clubs where interesting and worthwhile things are done.

A teacher knows students, protecting them rather than confronting them. Knowing a student doesn't mean having an academic history and a record of test scores. It means empathy—sensitivity to a student's interests, idiosyncracies, experience, preoccupations, preferences, and apprehensions.

A teacher should be an exemplar, not just to students and to other teachers, but to everyone who claims the authority to direct the course of education. Teachers must show what teaching is, for example by demonstrating that the prime purpose of education is not to be a proving ground for technology or a marketplace for entrepreneurs, but to provide interesting and supportive environments in which desirable activites will take place.

Not all learning is done in a face-to-face setting. Learners can identify with characters in books or with the authors of books. They can identify with characters in movies and videos. They can identify with people they encounter on computer networks. The role of classroom teachers is to ensure that students have opportunities to meet people worth identifying with, and to be able to enter enthusiastically into collaboration with them in order to learn what they are able to do.

Teaching on the Information Highway

Obviously, identification is possible through electronic networks, just as it is through books. The opportunities are almost endless—an interested student can eavesdrop upon and participate in the conversations of groups of astronomers, aviators, chefs, environmentalists, musicians, philosophers, zoologists, and everything between. The problem is not the experiences that technology offers teachers and students, provided they stay in control, but the opportunity for control the technology offers outsiders. Someone has to make choices about where the information highway leads, at one end of every possible interaction or the other. This again is what teachers are good for and should be employed for—providing and making choices.

I do not view the prospect of electronic education without apprehension. This is not because I don't see anything good coming from it. As countless individuals have already discovered, great personal, professional, social, intellectual, and even educational benefit can be found in excursions around the Internet. Experience in cyberspace can be satisfying (if not addictive). But the fact that anyone on the network can be a teacher doesn't mean that anyone should be.

I am not saying that the Internet should be kept out of the classroom —that won't be possible. But it should not be the means by which outside control is brought directly into the classroom.

The invasion may not be the result of a violent frontal assault. It can be a benign enterprise by well-intentioned people. In my own province of Canada, a group of local writers is working with the education ministry on a project called Putting Writers in the Classroom. The general idea is one that many people, myself included, have been advocating for years, that potential writers should be brought into contact with practicing ones. But the assumption has always been that teachers and writers would act together, or at least be responsive to each other. The current scheme has left teachers standing on the sidelines. On one side the ministry has recruited writers and other outsiders to help put in place a networking system (the first step of which, naturally, will be the construction of evaluation instruments). On the other side, the ministry is developing procedures to train teachers to adapt to the new technology. In effect, the teachers and writers are being kept at arm's length from each other as the network is organized.

The writer who gave me the news proclaimed, "We're getting into the classroom"—not, "We're being invited into the classroom," (at least not by teachers). What good is any innovation if teachers have little say about who comes into the classroom, when, how, and about the consequences? I was told that writers would participate in the ministry scheme as "representatives of the cultural industry." That is the way they are being slotted into the ministry blueprint. Many other industries are also participating. Are their representatives also celebrating "getting into the classroom"?

The Preservation of Teachers in the Information Age
Everyone should be concerned about how education will inevitably change as we move into a new age. But teachers must be *leaders*; they *must* be influential. They can't stop change, but they can try to take

charge of their own destiny, preserving their essential role in a changing world. There is no sign that any large or influential group of outsiders will step in to help teachers. Teachers must organize their own survival.

Teachers should not allow electronic technology to encroach on their domain, but they will not accomplish this by turning their backs. They must master the technology themselves—not a few "specialist teachers" but everyone, just as we have all had to come to terms with the technology of automobiles, television, credit cards, and banking machines.

Teachers will not survive if the world regards them as secondary to the information they are supposed to teach. All of those who think differently must be educated to reject the view that learning is information acquisition and that assessment and accountability are all that is required to ensure that teachers are doing their jobs.

Schools are social institutions, of a different and deeper order than the social organization of the information highway. There is a need to preserve schools as well as teachers, just as it could be argued that there is a social need for keeping workplaces, department stores, banks, and libraries. People should be able to meet face-to-face, or side by side, demonstrating the essential humanity of humankind.

Schools are important only to the extent that they facilitate face-to-face contact between learners and exemplars (given that face-to-face may sometimes mean book-to-face and even monitor-to-face, but never information-in-your-face). Administrators, trustees, politicians, and always parents can play a central role in ensuring that these contacts come about, not by imposing them directly, but by making them available for teachers and enabling teachers to make the ultimate choices.

My local supermarket is part of a chain that tries to operate under the concept of internal and external customers. External customers are those who come to the store to buy, the "clients." Internal customers are the people who work in the store to serve the external customers, but who are themselves the clients of suppliers and managers. It is recognized that internal customers must be content before external customers can be. The responsibility of management and suppliers is to serve the internal customers, to enable them to do their job, not to presume to do it for them, or to make it more difficult. Teachers have to consolidate their own position as internal clients of the educational system before they can be assured of providing the best service to the external clients, the students.

What kinds of examples should teachers provide? What are the kinds of things I have been calling "interesting" and "worthwhile"? A list could be endless—generalities like a love of learning, collaboration, independence, individuality, respect for others, and self-respect, and all kinds of specific topics: art, carpentry, cookery, drama, gardening, geography, histories, and music. A list would also be contentious, involving all kinds of family and community values and feelings.

It doesn't normally help for distant authorities or government departments to formulate curriculums. Any curriculum reflects values. The only parts of a predetermined curriculum that would be accepted globally are the ones that almost everyone would accept in any case, like literacy and mathematics (and even then there would be disagreement over the scope and content). Values are always diluted or degraded by attempts to standardize them.

Anything that would be divisive within a community would be even more divisive imposed centrally. This dilemma is another reason for the need for teachers to be influential. Teachers should be responsive to ideals and sensitivities in the localities in which they work. This is never easy, nor entirely feasible—but can authorities further away, geographically and philosophically, do better than teachers on the spot?

In the Long Run

I must admit that I have only been talking about the short run. The world is changing rapidly, and it would be futile to suggest that education can escape radical transformation, or to predict what the future will hold. It is not difficult to devise science-fiction scenarios. Perhaps in the long run the necessity I asserted for human beings to function face-to-face will prove incorrect, or illusory. Perhaps a posthuman future will be a world of electronic networks, not the information highway but the information cosmos, with individuals (or their brains) isolated and relatively inconsequential components of the system. Perhaps the network doesn't need us. All the more reason, I think, for teachers especially to demonstrate that we don't necessarily need the network.

Nobody could have foreseen where computers would take art, aviation, banking, or bureaucracies. No one can anticipate how the information highway will transform shopping, marketing, medicine, law, publishing, entertainment, and education—except that the developments will be fundamental. The developments are not merely technological—they are social, political, and existential.

It might be argued that if teachers as individuals are of such significance in education, why can't the same apply to actual or simulated teachers on the information highway? Can't "virtual teachers" take over from the flesh and blood variety? My answer—again in the long run—is that I don't know. Maybe this will be the inevitable end, and the only salaried human teachers left will be servicing the highway, not the students. Sooner or later, the technology will take us far beyond anything we might currently imagine.

Whatever the future, I don't want to get there too soon and too compliantly. We should not allow the information highway to be bulldozed precipitately into classrooms by corporate juggernauts, encouraged by high-level hitchhikers from the educational hierarchy. It should be admitted selectively and employed sensitively by discriminating teachers—demonstrating what they are good for.

Chapter 7

How Schools Must Change

The title to this essay is intentionally ambiguous. I am concerned with how schools *ought* to change, in order to make education more effective and worthwhile for students, teachers and society as a whole. But first I must talk about the only way schools *can* change, in any fundamental and lasting manner. In other words, I have two topics: the way in which schools change, for better or for worse, and the kind of change that we should aim for, a change for the better.

Changing schools is not a new idea, of course. Teachers are always trying to improve schools, and so are all kinds of authorities outside the classroom. Parents, employers, and other groups continually call for "better" schools. There is a great traffic in slogans about "excellence" or "quality" in education through improved programs, curriculums, objectives, goals, and evaluation. This is the way many teachers talk, and are expected to talk. But the aspirations behind all this talk are doomed to disappointment because any changes that result will be superficial. Education will not change with new and improved programs, curriculums, objectives, goals, or evaluation because these are the cause of many of the current problems. The improvement of education requires a different kind of language, a new way of looking at schools, and a better understanding of how change is brought about.

How Schools Change

Schools—and educational systems as a whole—are always changing, in *profound* and *superficial* ways. Profound changes make a real and lasting difference to teaching and to learning. They usually occur slowly, sometimes imperceptibly, although occasionally with violent suddenness. Superficial changes, on the other hand, are cosmetic. They give an immediate appearance of matters taken in hand, of progress being made, but in the long run they don't make the slightest difference. They are not worth the disruption they cause.

Profound changes affect the complex structure of social relationships within schools. They either improve education or they make it worse. To explain why the only changes that make a difference are those affecting the social structure of schools, I must first review briefly the nature of learning.

Learning and Schools

Learning is a social phenomenon. The simple fact that we learn from the company we keep has been recognized for over two thousand years. Children first learn to talk like their parents (or whoever else nurtures them), then like their friends. Whatever their genetic inheritance, and whatever their cultural background, children also learn to dress like their friends, to groom and ornament themselves like their friends, and to accept the values of their friends. The fact that we learn from the company we keep is implicitly recognized by all the parents who strive to send their children to schools populated by "the kind of people we are" (or that they have aspirations for their children to become).

Adults are not exempt from learning in this way. We all learn to be like the members of the groups—the "clubs"—with which we affiliate. We would not join these formal and informal associations if we did not see ourselves as being like the other members, and if the members did not see us as being like them. At the heart of the matter is *identity*, the question of who we are. And our identity is socially determined, decided for us by the people whose clubs we join, who accept us into their clubs (and also, negatively, by the people whose clubs we don't want to join, or who exclude us from their clubs). Experience—which primarily means our interactions with other people—teaches us who we are, what we can do, and what will always be closed to us.

The amount of learning accomplished in the course of personal interactions, by children and by adults, is enormous. It is also easy, unconscious, effortless, inconspicuous, and usually unplanned, by the learner and by the other club members, who "teach" by unwitting example. The only kind of learning that is difficult is "contrived" learning, where we make an effort to become something we don't see ourselves as being. Effortful learning, when we apply ourselves to the task, is likely to be difficult and in the long run certain to be unavailing (because rote learning is subject to rapid forgetting). Ironically, contrived learning, rather than the meaningful "incidental" learning of everyday life, has been most studied by experimental psychologists. Ironically also, it is the aspect of learning most focussed on in education.

The social basis of learning is typically disregarded in schools, where instruction is supposed to be "delivered" in an impartial or neutral setting, and intellectual effort rather than interpersonal relationships is expected to produce results. Students are required to learn from contrived materials, in isolation, by individual effort (even if cramped thirty or more to the classroom). Schools are commonly regarded as places where learning will take place if teachers and students perform properly. Failure to learn is attributed to inadequate effort, personal disability, wilfulness, or incompetence (on the part of students, teachers, or both). What is not recognized is that learning is never absent, and that students who fail to learn what teachers are expected to teach them are nevertheless learning. They learn that they cannot do what is being taught.

It is not coincidental that failure in school is socially predictable. The students who do worst typically come from outside the dominant population. This fact is universally recognized; "deprived," "underprivileged," or "disadvantaged" students are expected to do badly. The blame is usually placed on the students themselves, or on their home background, not on the social structure of the school. The students are "diagnosed" as unready for schooling, when in fact schools are unprepared for them. Shannon (1985) notes that these students have a far more difficult time in school than other students. They are engaged in activities that they don't understand, rushed, constantly interrupted, corrected, expected to fail, and given less assistance. Of course, they are less successful (a self-fulfilling prophesy). When "mainstream" students fail, lack of appropriate stimulation rather than lack of ability is more likely to be cited as the cause.

None of the difficulties of many students in school should be attributed to absence of learning. Learning takes place all the time, in school and out. The problem is never that students don't learn in school, but that they fail to learn what we hope they will learn, and they learn things we would rather they didn't. They may learn negative attitudes toward what they are supposed to be taught, toward school, toward the society that requires or urges them to attend educational institutions, toward their teachers, and toward themselves. Many of these attitudes involve social relationships, and all are affected in the course of social interactions. What makes a difference in schools is the way people relate to each other.

Profound Changes

Changes in the social structure of education permeate all aspects of school experience, from kindergarten to university. They affect the way teachers and students perceive themselves and each other. Changes in social climate result in profound differences to how teachers teach and to what students learn. Several such changes have occurred in the past hundred years.

The move from the one-room schoolhouse toward age and ability grouping at the end of the last century was a profound change. It transformed schools from communities, where everyone interacted and collaborated with everyone else, to institutions based on segregation and discrimination. Personal relationships were affected. Teacher attitudes to students changed, and so did student attitudes toward each other. Instead of learning the advantages of mutual assistance, students began to learn the importance of "keeping up," and, if possible, "getting ahead."

A second profound change was instituted at the beginning of the present century when education, in an endeavor to be "scientific," adopted experimental psychology's contrived and nonsense-based theory of learning. The notion that learning was accomplished through repetition and application rather than sense and assistance turned the teacher into a scorekeeper and warped the personal relationship between teacher and student. Teachers were expected to deliver learning, not to demonstrate it. It was with this profound change that education turned its back on the social nature of learning, believing instead that learning would result from rigorous instructional organization and planning.

These two radical changes were consolidated after the conclusion of the First World War by the wholesale adoption of mass testing techniques from the armed services, where they had been used to determine the most effective (from the services' point of view) occupation and rank for recruits. Testing introduced, or legitimized, discrimination in schools, as students were streamed into their appropriate groups and allocated their appropriate status. Learning became comparative and competitive. Relationships between students, and between students and teachers, became even more tenuous and stratified.

Since the Second World War, and especially since the onset of the space age, education has been profoundly affected by the introduction of a wide range of manipulative techniques. From systems analysis, behavioral engineering, management theory, and logistics have been drawn the detailed specification of learning objectives, standardized instruction, and the constant monitoring and evaluation of achievement. Education was transformed by what might politely be called a technology of planning (or more accurately a technology of control). Fundamental classroom decisions began to be made by people who could see neither the teachers nor the students involved—another profound change in the relationships among students and teachers (and between schools and society).

Education is currently beginning to feel the effects of another profound change through the influence of the relatively new discipline of cognitive science, which has become deeply involved in educational research and development. Cognitive science is concerned with the organization of knowledge, primarily as a means of developing computer systems capable of interacting directly with humans and of making "intelligent" decisions on their own. Programming computers to behave in these ways is seen as similar to the education of children. The new discipline has united psychologists, linguists, and philosophers with computer technicians and artificial intelligence experts. It has resulted in a view of the brain as an "information-processing device," learning as the "acquisition of knowledge," and thinking as "operations upon knowledge." Educational theorists have already uncritically adopted from cognitive science such concepts as "reasoning processes," "knowledge structures," and "executive procedures," not in electronic information systems, but in the human brain.

Superficial Changes

Superficial changes in education may be more immediately conspicuous than profound changes, but they do not affect the interpersonal relationships of students and teachers, and as a consequence have little effect on learning. They can range from the number of students in a classroom at one time to the provision of subsidized milk. Open classrooms were a superficial change (especially in the timorous way the idea was usually implemented) and so is the growing concern with curriculum (whose only occasional effect is to substitute and sometimes increase time-consuming activities). The movement toward "teacher accountability" (as if teachers ever had a free hand to do what they liked), and the perverse practice of publishing school test results, similarly make little difference to the way students and teachers interact, though they make everyone more anxious. These changes (or even just talking about them) may attract attention, and occasionally make marked differences in the day-to-day activities of teachers and students, sometimes facilitating but usually hindering what they do. But the changes do not have a profound effect because they rarely alter the way teachers and students work together. They do not, and cannot, make the improvements that are always claimed for them.

The new program and testing initiatives that are continually being announced, and the constant drive to augment or amend instructional objectives, must inevitably fail, as they have been failing for the past thirty years. They make no difference to the underlying social structures of schools. Changing the content of a curriculum, the nature of a test, or the wording of an inspirational slogan, can't in itself improve education.

Of course, "profound" and "superficial" are relative terms, opposite ends of a continuum. Some changes fall between the extremes—they may have some significant effects and other more trivial ones. School meals are an example. They can make a profound difference in schools where students might otherwise be hungry, but little difference elsewhere. Other changes have varying effects depending on how they are implemented. In some schools, "writing across the curriculum" created a liberating climate where writing became more meaningful, a collaboration between students and teachers, a profound and important change. Elsewhere, writing across the curriculum simply meant expecting every teacher to pounce on spelling and punctuation errors, an unfortunate but relatively trivial difference.

Making a Difference

Schools come in infinite variety. They are found in differing locations, with different philosophies and programs, with different kinds of plant and facilities, with students drawn from different populations, and with different levels of funding. None of these factors determines whether a particular school is a good one or not. The fundamental way in which our personal judgments are formed about whether a school would be a desirable place to teach in, or to send our children to, is the social climate— the way the administration treats the faculty, the way faculty respond to the students, and the way the students interact with one another.

Classrooms vary similarly. They may *look* different—teachers work in classrooms of different sizes, decorated in different ways, using different methods and materials—but these are all superficial matters that do not determine the quality of the class or the school. To judge a classroom or a school, you must see how the teachers and students spend their time there.

You can't predict from an empty classroom what the class is like. You can pick up only the slightest of clues from the arrangement and decoration of the classroom, and even from samples of student work. It is easy to be misled, to jump to wrong conclusions—for example, that a bright classroom, full of colorful posters and individual children's work, is a good one. This is just like visiting someone's workshop or kitchen, which may be clinically neat or a baffling shambles, and which tells us little about the quality of what is produced there.

Strangely enough, principals often show visitors only empty rooms, and teachers frequently like to display the decorations of their own classrooms, even when students are in the room. Empty classrooms are usually what parents see at open houses and parents' evenings. This is not because principals and teachers are anxious not to disturb students at work in classrooms—students are generally expected to stop what they are doing when a visitor arrives, and the public address system is a continual Orwellian intrusion. But many principals and teachers seem persuaded that what counts is the window dressing, the *appearance* of a classroom.

Yet we all know that some teachers are good teachers however poor the conditions might be, and that others are miserable teachers no matter how favorable the circumstances. I am not saying that poor conditions are acceptable—they obviously make life more difficult for teachers and for students. But they challenge rather than change the quality of good teachers, while the most favorable conditions never make a good teacher out of a bad one.

How Schools Ought to Change

The solution is simply stated—we must stop using the old and tired language of what schools should be *achieving*, of new and improved curriculums, objectives, and tests, and start talking about what schools should be *like*. We must talk of what people *do* and how they interact with each other. We will not be ready for the uncertain, rapidly changing world of the future with file cabinets of proposed new objectives, curriculums, and evaluation procedures, all to be implemented in the same old way. We won't be fit for the future primed by cheerleader incantations of "priorities," "commitments," "excellence," or even "relevance." We must recognize what makes a difference in schools, and ask ourselves what kind of *places* we want our schools to be.

Inquiry of this kind does not require expertise in systems engineering, program planning, or curriculum theory. It requires sensitivities more like those of a novelist than those of a manager. It demands facility in creative thinking and descriptive writing which teachers and students might develop together, to the advantage of writing, reading, and thinking generally. The emphasis has to be on activities that people are free to do, not in terms of a prescribed list but in ways of bringing people together. It is not possible to specify what these activities should be, in fact specification would be against the spirit of the change. Metaphors are more appropriate, though none is exact. Schools should be like supermarkets (in terms of choice), emporia (in terms of animation), libraries and museums (in terms of access), newsrooms, theaters and artists' collectives (in terms of excitement) ocean liners (in terms of voyages), retreats (in terms of tranquility), villages, islands, communes, sanctuaries, guilds, clubs. . . . The possibilities are endless, and never complete. Schools should reflect every creative possibility.

We must get away from the idea that the function of schools is to teach and test skills and facts. Skills and facts are not learning, even if they seem to be the easiest things for teachers to teach and for tests to test. Learning is doing things: exploring, searching, selecting, experiencing, wondering, suspecting, challenging, building, arguing. The facts we gather are by-products of experience and imagination, not their cause. Learning is vocations, ideals, aspirations, fantasy, ideas, friendship, excitement, apprenticeship, play, hobbies, sport; it is musicians, writers, painters, thinkers, arguers, carpenters, sailors, cyclists, farmers, makeup artists, mothers, fathers, mentors, tool users, toolmakers, dreamers. Students should no more go to school—or to a university—to acquire knowledge than they would go to the gymnasium for the food and drink that will be the basis of their physical powers. The gymnasium is for the exercise of the body and the engagement of physical powers. The intellectual part of school should be for the exercise of the brain and the engagement of the imagination. Schools should be *interesting* places, for everyone in them.

I have previously listed four elements of ideal classroom "enterprises": (1) the elimination of grades, marks, and scores (which stigmatize any activity as a school ritual), (2) the banishment of coercion and discrimination, (3) freedom from artificial restrictions of the classroom walls or the daily timetable, and (4) removal of special status for teachers (Smith 1986). All would ameliorate the social climate of classrooms, enhancing possibilities for personal interaction.

There is one key word—*respect*. Ideal school situations exist when everyone has respect for what is being done and for the people it is being done with. Good teachers respect what they teach and they respect their students. They do not exploit their subject matter or their students in order to accomplish an educational objective or to implement an evaluative procedure. Good teachers are characterized not by their qualifications, their lesson plans, or even their activities, but by their *attitudes*, the role they perceive for themselves in the social fabric of the classroom.

Bringing About Change

We must get away from the idea that everything is fundamentally well with our educational institutions and that they only need patching up a bit. That is why we should no longer talk about schools in the language that has made them what they are. Schools, which were initially supposed to solve problems, are now the source of problems. Consolidating the way they are will make them worse. We must stop believing that we only need to make things a little better and everything will be fine. Education is on the wrong track, largely because of profound changes like those I have already enumerated which have socially isolated teachers from parents, students, and each other, making them cogs in an educational machine.

How should the change be brought about? The first answer must be, a little at a time. The world will not be changed overnight—and it is time education got realistic. But immediate change is not essential. Worthwhile situations already exist, perhaps in the majority of classrooms—some of the time. We need more of them (though no one needs ideal conditions all the time, and children especially are remarkably resilient to nonsense and to obstacles—as long as they are not persuaded that the triviality and irritations are important). Perhaps even more immediately important than the extension of worthwhile situations is more *recognition* of what they are.

The change could begin with collaborative inquiries by teachers and students into the nature of the educational system they are personally involved in, and what it does to student perceptions and attitudes. There could be honesty about the things which can't at the moment be changed but which should be changed.

Professional action will be required, a matter of education. Teachers must teach themselves, each other, their supervisors, their students, parents, politicians, and the world in general what good things can be done in schools. Such educating is most effectively done by demonstration, not exhortation. Classrooms must be opened to critics, and to the people whose attitudes teachers want to change. Changing attitudes is also a social rather than an intellectual matter. "Information" does not often make people change their ways; it often makes them dig in their heels. Even administrators need support, and the reassurance that their world will not collapse if they change their way of thinking, or permit teachers to change theirs.

There is a crucial need for support for teachers themselves—from students, parents, and especially administrators. Administrators should be a buffer between teachers and outside pressures, not the conduit by which external pressures are imposed on teachers. Schools can only be as strong as their teachers. There is perhaps too much focus in school reform on students and their performance. This puts an unfair and unmanageable burden on students, who are forced to be in school in the first place. The emphasis should be shifted to teachers—not on mythical performance levels and irrelevant measures of "accountability," but on their conditions of employment. Better and more effective schools would be places where teachers are able to do their traditional work of inspiring and assisting the young without harassment. Teachers must be trusted to teach, to find the most appropriate ways to teach, and to monitor their own profession. Schools should be more collegial. Teachers need more respect—from politicians and parents, from administrators, and from students. They lack respect from all these perspectives largely because of the managerial role that has been allocated to them, and its effect on their personal relationships with many of their students.

Two Current Profound Issues

Two changes which will make a profound difference to education are currently taking place in many schools. They are profound because they produce differences in the social structure of schools, and will inevitably lead to a reconsideration of the value of standardized instruction and testing. Both are widely regarded as "problems"—but they are really opportunities.

The first change is commonly known as "integration" (a term whose political connotations should not be ignored). The aim is to bring into classrooms students who would otherwise be segregated, generally students labelled "handicapped" or "different." Typical arguments against integration are that it imposes a great burden on regular classroom teachers, and that both "mainstream" and "challenged" students will suffer, the former by being held back and the latter by being pushed faster or further than they can go.

Teachers of integrated classrooms certainly need additional help— not with the handicapped students but with the class as a whole. The "coping" problem is not insoluble, especially if the barriers of the timetable and the classroom walls are made a little more permeable. One obvious source of help would be all the special education teachers and other personnel at present working with segregated students. The "holding back" and "pushing ahead" difficulties are both part of the larger social problems of competitiveness and standardization in education. But on the issue of whether education in general would suffer I would like to tell a story.

A few years ago I was invited to a school especially designed and run for the education of handicapped students. Nowhere else have I seen such a beautiful and well-equipped school. Everything was done with the needs of the students in mind. Ramps and handrails ran down into the expansive swimming pool, and the library, cafeteria, and classrooms were constructed from the perspective of occupants of wheelchairs. When one of the teachers asked me what I thought of the school, I said it was impressive. The teacher nodded—and then told me, "All this is conscience money. It's a way of hiding the students away. When they leave here, it's the end of their lives." When the students graduated, the teacher said, they hadn't learned how to live with the rest of society, and the rest of society hadn't learned how to live with them. Will education really suffer if the segregation of handicapped people is ended?

More recently, I was invited to talk at a conference on what was called "The problem of multiculturalism." The "problem" was the growing number of students from varying cultural backgrounds sharing the same classrooms—a second profound change that is already affecting large numbers of schools in dramatic ways.

I talked with some of the students involved and was struck by the deep pride and respect they had for their own cultures. It occurred to me that contemporary mainstream North America (and those countries that emulate it) might be unique in being the only culture that had succeeded in despoiling its own educational system—fouling its own nest—to the extent that its schools no longer worked in favor of the culture as the whole. They were divisive rather than cohesive.

But if that was the case, then a remedy could be at hand. Contemporary mainstream education must learn from cultures whose educational practices are still supportive and consolidating forces. And representatives of many of those cultures are already in our classrooms—the "problems" could be potential solutions. If teachers and students must explore education together, how better to do so than with students with a variety of backgrounds and perspectives?

"It Won't Work"

The suggestion that profound changes must be made to the social structure of schools invites all manner of queries and criticisms, many of which boil down to the simple reaction, "It won't work." Here are outlines of a few common reactions, and my responses to them.

"You're not being realistic"

This objection usually means that my comments don't fit into the way the educational system is organized. Schools currently run on objectives, tests, goals, and so forth; therefore, changes must be formulated in those terms. But it's the real world that I'm talking about, the way people actually learn. It may be difficult to change the nature of schools, but it's impossible to change the nature of people. Schools *must* change if education is to improve.

"Teachers can't do this with thirty students in the classroom"

It may be more difficult to have a productive social climate with thirty or more students in the classroom (compared with fifteen, for example), but that is no excuse for ignoring the personal interrelationships and social development of thirty students. I agree there should often be fewer students (though I would rather see one room with thirty students and two teachers than two rooms, each with fifteen students and one teacher). But however many students there are, their life and that of their teachers will be easier, and everyone will learn more, if the day's activities are based on flexibility and interpersonal relations—everyone helping everyone else—than on rigidity and control.

"We have to have standardization"
Children move from one school to another. How will their new teachers know where they are; how will they be able to keep up? The objection is based on the presupposition that specific items of learning have to be planned and taken in sequence. When it is acknowledged that the basis for learning is an interesting and collaborative environment, moving from one school to another could be regarded as an advantageous educational opportunity. Adults who travel extensively are not usually seen as being at intellectual risk. Standardization mitigates against everyone; it is another destructive rigidity. It's surprising how adapted we've become to the term in education. If a bureaucrat proposed to standardize the food we eat, or the cars we drive, or the clothes we wear (in the interests of economy, efficiency, and excellence, of course) there'd be a revolt.

On the other hand, "individualized" instruction has to be watched. It is not the opposite of standardization. Allowing students to "work at their own pace" through the same or different arbitrarily contrived materials still shows no respect for students or what they are expected to learn. Instead of competing against others, students compete against themselves.

The question of standardized requirements and evaluation procedures for *entry* into university, or certain occupations, is another issue. Even if such standardization is required, or even desirable, there is no justification for imposing inappropriate and stultifying rigidity on everyone. As for "standards" generally, they are best achieved without standardization.

"Teachers must have a curriculum"
The argument is that if teachers don't have a set of directions to follow, they won't know what to do. They need guidance. The argument is an insult to teachers, or to the systems that employ them. Teachers should not be expected to teach something they know nothing about, nor should they try to. Skilled teachers are not those who can "teach anything." On the other hand, teachers should be able to teach anything they are *interested* in learning themselves. The very things they have to do for their own learning—and the consideration and assistance they might claim from their students—could facilitate everyone's learning.

There is nothing wrong with general expectations about what teachers should teach, although these expectations are not always well expressed. It would be better to require that teachers *interest* students in reading, writing, mathematics, science, and other "subjects" than that students should learn them. Learning is far more likely with an interested student, and demands that teachers promote interest are less liable to be reduced to fragmented, decontextualized, and testable units than lists of specific knowledge and skills. It is better to interest students in some aspect of science, so that they come to think like scientists, than to try to teach a superficial and distorted smattering of many aspects of science.

"Schools reflect the real world"

The assertion here is that in the greater society outside school everyone has objectives, competition is rife and evaluation a constant fact of life, so why should schools be different? But all of these assertions are false.

Individuals have goals or aims (which may be called objectives), but they are more in the nature of aspirations or directions than a ladder of obstacles that must be overcome. We set personal objectives for ourselves (which does not mean that children should be coerced or cajoled into setting "educational objectives" for themselves, any more than they should be made "responsible" for their own learning). Failure to achieve a personal objective is more an occasion for commiseration and help than for denunciation and ostracism. We are unlikely to be told that we are disabled, or need to shape up, or that we have "special needs." Employers who specify objectives for workers are either enraptured by the latest motivational jargon or exploiters of labor. Individual competitiveness in the world outside school is largely limited to sports, and a matter of voluntary participation. Industrial and commercial companies compete—but their motives are crass and usually fail to infect their workers.

Evaluation, where it does occur in the outside world, usually results in those who can't do something well receiving assistance, not condemnation. The world at large is inordinately tolerant of incompetence. Most government, industrial, and commercial concerns (and universities) carry a large number of passengers whose work is done for them by their colleagues or subordinates. Incompetence is widely protected, by unions, professional associations, fellow workers, friends, and families. Only in schools, which take the lead in discriminatory practices, are those who fail to meet expectations pilloried.

Besides, even if objectives, competitiveness, and evaluation were rampant in the world outside school, why should they dominate school as well? They don't promote worthwhile learning. Why shouldn't schools be sanctuaries?

"What does 'better,' 'improved,' or 'more effective' schools mean?"

I can't say what other people have in mind, but I have a simple, almost platitudinous point of view. Schools are better and more effective when everyone finds being in them worthwhile, and people would be there even if they were not paid or coerced. They are places where worthwhile learning occurs because everyone wants to participate in what is going on, teachers don't get burned out, administrators don't feel beleaguered, and students are not harassed. They are places where respect is taught, not as a subject on the curriculum, but as the spirit of the institution itself—respect for the world, for all people in it, for ideas, for learning, for open-mindedness, for tolerance, and for the creative powers and products of the human mind. I don't think I am talking about anything that is impossible—only something that must be universally claimed as a right for teachers and students.

Chapter 8

Research: Getting on Top and Out from Under

A traumatic moment occurs for many new teachers—and often for more experienced ones—when someone tells them that everything they believe about teaching reading and writing is false.

Graduating student teachers may discover that what they have so conscientiously studied is widely regarded as misguided if not dangerous. They may have gone through their entire education without being warned that sooner or later they would be challenged by colleagues, administrators, and parents holding contrary points of view. Even teachers who have taught for many years may find themselves wondering if they have been doing the right thing for all that time.

When teachers eventually encounter an opposing point of view, it may be presented with evangelical fervor while their own beliefs and practices are denounced and ridiculed. And they may find little solace if they consult research journals, attend conferences, or seek the opinion of "experts." Questions that might seem relatively simple, such as whether spelling should be formally taught, worksheets employed, errors corrected, or tests administered, become polarizing battle lines. Teachers can find themselves expected to take a position and to defend it.

I am referring to the dilemma of teachers pitched precipitately into literacy's "Never-Ending Debate" (see Chapter 4 of this book). In that essay, I propose that the fiercely rival points of view about how reading and writing should be taught are based on deeply held ideological beliefs. The "debate" will never be resolved by research and rarely be assuaged by reason on the part of either side.

Nevertheless, many people inside the classroom and out retain the faith that research should ultimately and irrefutably prove one side right and the other wrong. In fact, many people—again on both sides—are convinced that the issue *has been* settled, that the relevant research has been done and that all the necessary evidence is in. This view is especially strongly held by the researchers themselves.

I shall briefly examine—particularly from an educational point of view—the nature of research, some reasons why it is undertaken, the confusions it can create, how teachers can avoid being overwhelmed by it, and how they can nevertheless usefully engage in it themselves. Research is essential, though it will never be perfect, and I encourage teachers to take part in it. Every educator should be able to approach research without bewilderment or despondency.

The Nature of Research

Research is not the same thing as curiosity (though it may be fueled by curiosity) because it is rarely open to seeing, let alone accepting, everything that might be revealed. It is not the same thing as investigation (though it may be part of an investigation) because it is frequently reluctant to follow where evidence leads. Research is too systematized to be open-minded. The outcome of research is not supposed to be surprising, and should be unambiguously connected to the hypotheses the researchers carry into their inquiries. Research that meets the expectations of a researcher's peers is more likely to be published than research with unexpected or tendentious results.

There are basically two different ways of doing research—or "paradigms"—which might be broadly characterized as *experimental* and *descriptive*.

The *experimental* approach requires the manipulation of situations so that arbitrarily established states of affairs can be compared with each other or with states of affairs that have not been deliberately constructed. The manipulation is often referred to as a "treatment," and the essence of the procedure is to ensure that the only evident difference between the situations or individuals being compared is the presence or absence of a treatment. In that way, any difference that transpires can be attributed to the treatment, which becomes in effect a question: "What difference does this treatment make?" A typical piece of experimental educational research compares outcomes when one group of students is given a particular kind of instruction and another is not. The feelings and perceptions of the individuals involved—the "subjects"—would normally be considered "extraneous variables," less relevant than their "performance," or test scores. The experimental approach is also termed "scientific" or "objective." It can usually be identified in its publications by the conspicuous use of statistical tests of significance.

The opposing *descriptive* approach typically refrains from making comparisons or applying treatments, but instead attempts to observe and fully describe what is going on in a particular situation. The descriptive approach would, for instance, attempt to analyze in great depth and detail the dynamics of a classroom when a new instructional procedure is introduced, from individual and social points of view. The personal perceptions of the individuals involved in the situation would be taken into account. The descriptive approach may also be referred to as "naturalistic," "observational," "clinical," or "ethnographic." Its publications could contain summary data in tabular form but rarely statistical analyses.

The two research paradigms are so dissimilar that people who follow one approach very often don't regard people who follow the other as legitimate researchers at all. Experimentalists hold that reliable answers can't be found unless all aspects of a situation are rigorously controlled. They regard descriptive techniques as subjective, asserting that the beliefs and behaviors of people can be observed, analyzed, and described in any arbitrary kind of way, and also that it is impossible for any situation to be exhaustively described. Experimentalists employ a number of unflattering terms to characterize descriptive research: "anecdotal," "armchair philosophizing," and "handwaving" are among the more polite. They attempt to refute descriptive arguments by asking for evidence.

Descriptive researchers, on the other hand, claim that only their approach can examine situations "authentically," not as the researcher desires or arranges them to be. They maintain that the experimental approach is artificial and intrusive, so narrowly focussed that experimenters can ignore important things going on in front of their noses. They also use terms like "mechanistic," "deterministic," and "reductionist." Descriptive researchers attempt to refute experimental conclusions by asking whether they make sense.

The two approaches can be found in almost all fields of inquiry, and there are no irrefutable grounds for asserting that one paradigm is essentially more valid or relevant than the other, though there are plenty of partisan arguments. One approach may be easier than the other in particular circumstances. Each approach needs a different kind of professional preparation, and often external circumstances and even historical accident will determine the kind of research a particular researcher will tend to do. Personality characteristics doubtless play an important role as well.

Researchers frequently do all of their research in just one of the two paradigms. Some move from one kind of research to the other, but relatively few engage in both, or attach the same significance to both.

There is no point in asking which approach is better, or more appropriate, even in specific circumstances. Proponents of the two paradigms will give different answers. And there is no point in wondering which side will ultimately prevail. A unified perspective among researchers is about as likely as unanimity in religion or politics. The fact that there will be endless argument in research and about research is something we must all live with. Education students should have been told about the uncertainty and antagonism with their first introduction to a research topic. Research always aims to answer questions, but the questions are never ones that everyone agrees should be asked.

Why Research Is Done

There is a romantic notion that all research is undertaken with one noble end in mind—to add unambiguously to our store of knowledge. However, a good deal of research of both kinds is done not to answer burning questions but to fulfil the demands of a course of study, the requirements of a job, or the predilections of a funding agency. Research is often a ritual, if not a trial. Many people do research who would rather not, and look forward to the time when they need not do it any more, just as a good deal of academic publishing is done not because people have something to say but because they need the authorial credit. Professors must "publish or perish."

There is a temptation to join research bandwagons—the easiest way for someone without a publication history to get published. Graduate students look for topics that will be acceptable and manageable. Rather than being driven to find answers to problems that personally concern them, their greatest problem is often to find a topic that will enable them to get a requirement out of the way. They are often advised to do something not very different from what others have done before, since innovative research complicates the lives of students, supervisors, and examining committees. The line of research that many professional researchers follow through their lives may be directly derived from the "research program" of the professor who happened to supervise their dissertation. Other researchers follow topics and procedures determined by where they manage to find funds, until necessity nudges them in some other direction.

I am not saying that people who do research have superficial attitudes toward it. Research is frequently tedious and time-consuming, requiring great dedication to be carried through to completion. Proposal and report writing can be a chore, and submission for publication invites criticism, frustration, and rejection. Published researchers risk public identification with particular schools of thought. As a consequence, some researchers develop intense commitment to their topic, methodology, and conclusions. They become blind to alternatives, dogmatic in debate and hostile in confrontation. Not every participant in research resembles this bleak characterization, of course, but the field is a competitive one in which goodwill and self-effacement don't naturally thrive.

Research is a shibboleth of our time, and being a researcher is usually rated above being a practitioner or teacher, whose experience "on the job" or "in the field" may be denigrated as particularly untrustworthy, a handicap rather than an advantage. People who have done little or no research themselves are sometimes eager to be identified with it. In promoting the latest trend in anything from diet to neuroscience they will say "we know . . . ," or "we have found . . . ," rather than "research shows . . . ," or (better) "research indicates . . . ," "research suggests . . . ," or "researchers claim. . . ."

Why Research May Be Confusing

I have already indicated a major reason why turning to "the research" to find straightforward answers to questions can be such an inconclusive and unsatisfying experience. Research is inherently quarrelsome, and the deeper it is probed, the more contention is likely to be revealed. Critical contradictions between theoretical positions are quickly uncovered, and then large numbers of researchers will be found enthusiastically supporting one side and excoriating the other. Arguments will be found that both sides are wrong, or—perhaps worse—that both sides are right. The one thing unlikely to be disclosed is doubt. Research almost invariably begins and ends with rock solid certitude on the part of the researchers that the right things were done and the right conclusions drawn. Only outsiders have misgivings.

There is a second reason for the massive frustration of research: There is so much of it. An impossible amount of it! I'm talking of inundation. To attempt to read all the research related to reading or writing would be a Sisyphean (or Augean) enterprise, even if restricted to the publications of just a single year. The flood of research does not bring increasing returns, only increasing confusion.

Well over 1000 research studies are abstracted every year in the International Reading Association's *Annual Summary of Investigations*

Related to Reading. Over 18,000 articles on writing were listed in the ERIC registry between 1980 and 1989 (Farnan, Lapp, and Flood 1992), and over 160 writing projects were set up in the United States during the decade. The net result, according to the authors, was no increase in the amount of writing done in schools.

When I prepared a fifth edition of *Understanding Reading* in 1994, my expeditions into mountains of research found little that was new since the first edition was published in 1971. The main research controversies had persisted for a quarter of a century (what it means to be a reader, how written words are recognized, and how reading should be taught), and basic theoretical positions had hardened rather than changed. Even some of the major protagonists were the same (including myself), all significantly older but not noticeably more conciliatory.

Did I say mountains of research? I calculated that in preparing the fifth edition I spent about twenty months examining over 2000 research reports (and sidestepping at least 20,000 others). I cited about 200 of them. It was not a labor I would recommend to anyone, yet there are scholars who spend large parts of their lives diligently *doing research on research*. Hillocks (1986), for example, reviewed 6000 research studies on composition, summarizing 2000 of them. Such monumental efforts only confirm (and augment) the daunting barricades of published research confronting those who would try to surmount them.

There is more evidence about teaching literacy than anyone knows what to do with, coming raw into educational theorizing and policy making, to be processed in different ways for different purposes by people with different agendas and different points of view. Research is used to promote instructional methodologies, political propensities, and pedagogical dogmas. The fact that a product or program is "research-based" (as well as "new") can inflame educational authorities desperate to find anyone who can claim instructional innovation with "demonstrated results."

Educational research is almost bound to be dogmatic and confrontational. After all, it pertains to children and to education, subjects that most people feel strongly about. It also pertains to our own behavior and beliefs, about which we may feel even more keenly. Our careers may depend on it—and so may the careers of the researchers. Research that admits to uncertainty is unlikely to be published. Research that fails is rarely reported, yet it might be more revealing than the research that is a "success."

The fact that research may be inconclusive, unreliable, and even wrong creates great difficulties for some people. Some hold to a rosy belief that science is an incremental activity—that every bit of research is valid and worthwhile, adding a nugget of truth to a growing accumulation of knowledge and understanding. All reported findings are supposed to fit together like pieces of a jigsaw puzzle, no matter how contradictory they might appear. Educational textbooks are frequently pastiches of this nature, covering immense amounts of ground without the provision of navigable pathways.

Another common response is to ignore the possibility that conventionally held positions might have been discredited and to attempt instead to assimilate alternative points of view into established or "official" lines of thinking. Conceptual mixing and matching is frequently found in research summaries produced by committees or by bureaucratic institutions. A prominent example is *Becoming a Nation of Readers: The Report of the Commission on Reading,* published by the federally-funded Center for the Study of Reading at the University of Illinois (Anderson et al. 1985). The report cites—and even recommends—a variety of irreconcilable points of view about how reading is learned and should be taught.

How to Escape Inundation

We live in diluvian times, awash in all kinds of "information." So how can a teacher, or a student, cope with the flood of research that threatens to inundate education? There can be no definitive answer—but then, part of the problem is that so much research is produced and promoted by people who believe there *are* definitive answers, and that they have them. Doubt is the life raft that can enable readers to navigate the broad reaches of research—or to get out from under the tidal wave.

I am not saying it is necessary to be open-minded in going into research. That would hardly be practical. Anyone who could be totally open-minded, with no prior point of view, would have no way of escaping confusion. The trick is to get a purchase on the research, to relate it to ideas and states of affairs that are personally relevant.

If asked, I sometimes recommend that teachers begin with research on themselves, examining their own practices and points of view. All their behavior, and their attitudes and beliefs, in school and out, are based on assumptions, on what they take for granted. I suggest they imagine having to justify everything they do to a rather hostile interrogator, or to a skeptical student. These may not be the best analogies, since there are temptations to dissimulate in intimidating circumstances. An alternative is to imagine *they* are the interrogators, uncovering the fundamental beliefs of someone who happens to teach exactly the way they themselves do.

All that might sound insuperably difficult. The next hint is a little easier. I don't ask teachers to doubt and defend their own position when they go into the research. Instead I suggest that they doubt and attack the research, from the position they have established for themselves. I recommend constantly asking if they believe what they are reading, and if it makes sense to them. And if they feel themselves being carried along in a rosy haze of concord, because it is all so congenial and persuasive, they might take a closer look to see what is creating that effect. The most effective selling techniques strive to enlist the support of potential customers before they even realize what they are being sold.

Here are other suggestions I sometimes offer.

- Don't venture into the research without a good reason (though purposeful browsing can also be an interesting and productive activity). Go in to see what is said that is directly of concern to you. And go in *aggressively*—be argumentative. Exercise some consumer resistance.
- Don't expect a consensus; people have different points of view. Don't allow anyone to make your decisions for you. Don't just read the discussion and conclusion—examine what the researcher was looking for. In particular, try to work through the methodology section (a part of research readers often skip). Imagine yourself a subject of the research, and ask how the requirements of the researcher relate to actual situations that you are familiar with.
- Try to see how different researchers come to totally contrary points of view; note the procedures they follow, the logic they employ. Compare their tracks as well as their conclusions.
- Much of the research and argumentation is repetitious, and the probability that you will miss something critical—that some dramatic discovery will drift past you without your hearing about it—is essentially zero. It is not difficult for teachers to find out what the research—and the issues—are about. Ask other people (some you agree with and some you don't) what they find to be important sources. Alternatively, focus on the professional journals that are supposed to be relevant to your particular areas of concern. Either way, don't stop at the front line, the store front, but go back to the sources that are cited to support the articles that you read. Who are the authorities that the authorities rely on?
- Don't be intimidated by the number of references. Exhaustive recapitulation of everything anyone might have said on any aspect of the topic is tedious in theses (though often demanded by professors) and unnecessary in other publications. Fiske and Campbell (1992) pointedly observe that citations don't solve problems, and Vincente and Brewer (1993) note that

quoted research has often been read and cited inappropriately because of theoretical bias. Cronbach (1992) also warns that the presence of a large number of citations in a research article does not mean that intended messages have been understood. There is a great temptation for authors of research reports to cite secondary sources—to quote people who quote other people—without checking whether the intermediaries have got it right. Even more misleadingly, the original sources cited by secondary sources may be cited directly even though they haven't been seen or closely examined—a totally illegitimate practice that could be as widespread and even understandable as fudging on tax returns.

- Don't be impressed by names. Even eminent scientists may have difficulty seeing research results and opposing arguments objectively. They are supposed to be open-minded and impartial, but they often have a great deal at stake, personally and professionally, in the outcome of research. They may not be able to afford to hold a discredited position, or to appear to vacillate, therefore their approach has to be beyond criticism. Quite unintentionally, they may be far more obdurate than people without scientific allegiance or pretension.
- Don't restrict yourself to major national and international research journals. Some of the most important research for any teacher might be done by a colleague in a neighboring classroom or school, and published in a regional journal. What "local research" may lack in scholarly detachment it can make up for in relevance.
- All these strictures may seem to present an enormous burden, so here's a piece of practical advice: Don't try to do any of this alone. Everything I have mentioned—analyzing your own beliefs, getting into the research, being selective, resisting the sales pitches, and even changing your views and behavior, will be far easier if you don't try to do it in isolation. Find allies. You need other people for assistance and support. Start or join a discussion group where you don't all read the same thing but examine as wide a range of research as possible. The Internet can be invaluable here. The world is full of people who find educational research inadequate, confusing, and overwhelming. Collaboration is crucial in every aspect of education.

What about teachers who are so biased that they could never see merit in any fresh point of view that they encounter? Sorry, but I'm not offering miracles. No one wins *all* the time.

But I don't object to hard-nosed attitudes on the part of readers. For many people, there is an authority about the written word that ought to be resisted. Published research—and educational theorizing—may be given more credence than it deserves because we assume that no one would knowingly disseminate something that is unsubstantiated or incorrect. And it is all too easy to be convinced by printed material that appeals directly to our beliefs or soothes our apprehensions.

Everything I have said about reading published research may apply even more to *hearing* about it from advocates at conferences, seminars, and workshops. When an audience is present it is easy for listeners *and* speakers to be carried away. This is one reason I think that important work at any conference is done in the intervals between presentations, though they are often too brief and infrequent. Participants need time to talk to each other and to themselves. Reason requires reflection.

After all these cautions I should perhaps reiterate that I'm not against research. We might have too much of it, but I wouldn't want anyone to legislate which part we could do without. I'm simply saying that research should not be regarded as infallible and sacrosanct. Research is like art or music—we all have somewhat different tastes, can approach it in various ways, and be affected by it differently. Nevertheless, research is essential, and everyone in education should do it, knowingly and deliberately. We should all engage in research to find some of our own answers, and also because the greatest defense against being overwhelmed by the sheer bulk and intransigence of other people's research is being active and useful members of the researchers' club ourselves.

How to Be a Useful Researcher

Research as I have described it may have seemed a dismal and even foolhardy pursuit, with anyone who engages in it likely to become trapped in futility and dissention. But there is a way to get on top of research, and that is to make it personal.

The key is reader involvement by relating it always to one's own situation. Readers make relevance possible—and detect irrelevance—by bringing a frame of mind with them. Teachers should be researchers so that they can make their own decisions about their own classrooms and engage in productive discussion with colleagues, but not necessarily to add to some great but mythical common pool of incontrovertible research findings. All teachers should engage in research themselves so that they have some standing when they turn to the judgments of more professional researchers.

The best way for practicing teachers to make sense of research on any topic related to education is to examine issues first in their own class-rooms and neighborhoods. I don't aim to provide a research manual for teachers at this point—there are plenty of them around. Instead, here are five considerations that I think are critical whether we are doing the research ourselves or scrutinizing the research of others—whether it is purposeful, relevant, coherent, clear, and sensible.

- *Purposeful*: Research should be done for a good reason, clearly specified. This doesn't mean there is no need for "pure" research without any obvious immediate practical application. But there should be a place where the research fits, where it becomes worth doing and examining. It is not meretricious.
- *Relevant*: The nature of the research should follow from the reason it is done. The procedures or methodology shouldn't diverge into something else, no matter how ingenious they might appear.
- *Coherent*: Each part of the research and the report on it should fit with every other part. There should be no extraneous interpolations or disconcerting omissions.
- *Clear*: Readers should not have to struggle to understand what the researcher has done.
- *Sensible*: Readers should not have to struggle to believe what the researcher reports. The results may be surprising, but they should not be incredible. They should at least have surface validity.

I'm tempted to add a sixth virtue, *brevity*. Reports that demand so much time, concentration, and effort that readers will be inclined to give up before even getting into them make little contribution.

There is a particular reason why teachers should engage in what might be called *local research*, especially on matters relevant to their own classrooms, schools, and communities. They should find their own questions and their own ways of answering them, looking at what people in similar situations have done and replicating it in their own circumstances. Findings and conclusions should be publicized among peers and other interested people, perhaps even by starting a local research journal or computer network.

Why do I stress the local? Because the results or conclusions of generalized research should rarely be applied directly to specific situations. There are always personal and social variables that "universalized" research cannot take into account.

And conversely, it is inadvisable to leap to generalization from local results, when it may not be possible or desirable to apply all the usual textbook rules about validity, verification, and replication in research. On the other hand, the most useful and relevant kind of research may often be local, not universal.

Local research should not be disparaged. It could be argued that there are only local truths in education. Everything must be put in context. A bullheaded drive for universal generalizations about teaching and learning may be both fruitless and unnecessary. But research leading to chaos theory has demonstrated that even in universes that churn with incomprehensible turbulence, local regions of harmony and predictability may form and flourish.

Chapter 9

Let's Declare Education a Disaster (and Get On with Our Lives)

I have a serious suggestion to make. We should stop worrying about the problems of education, declare it a disaster, and let teachers and students get on with their lives.

The trouble with the endless concern over "problems" in education is that many well-meaning but often misguided and sometimes meddlesome people believe solutions must exist. They waste their own and other people's time and energy trying to find and implement these solutions. Typically they try harder to do more of something that is already being done, although what is being done is probably one of the problems. If education is a disaster then it is not a collection of problems that can be "solved," and trying to "improve" what we are already doing will only make the situation worse. You don't find solutions to disasters—you try to extricate yourself and other people from them. The way to survive a disaster is to do something different.

When the *Titanic* hit the iceberg the people aboard had a problem: the vessel was leaking. They could try to solve this problem by making the ship watertight again and continuing the voyage. But when the *Titanic* began irrevocably to sink, they had a disaster. They had to try to get everyone away in lifeboats—something they would have done better had they turned their backs on their leakage problem sooner and concentrated on saving themselves and each other.

Education is not the only condition of our lives that should be regarded as a disaster rather than a set of problems. The environment, the economy, health care, arms proliferation, universal hunger, drug abuse, and the state of our cities are a few other instances that spring easily to mind. To take just one example, politicians promise to attack "the problems" of the economy—or of the deficit, or of unemployment —with all kinds of solutions. The promises are never fulfilled. Whatever politicians do—or don't do—the situation persists, or gets worse, unless chance circumstances temporarily make it better.

I don't claim to be an economist, so I have no solutions to propose. But you don't need to be a doctor to know when someone is sick. And all the technical expertise in the world won't help when the patient is dead. I don't think our economic dilemmas can be solved, certainly not the way anyone currently in charge is trying to solve them. Economists have been attacking problems of the economy for years, and the economy has been getting worse. The economy is a disaster. Economists are always ready to blame someone else (even each other) for the chronic mess. But some at least must have been responsible for where we are today, unless the economy is out of their control, in which case economists can't do anything about it and should give up saying they can.

Why do we think there must be "solutions" to so many of life's most conspicuous difficulties? Why do we try so perversely to teach problem solving in our problem-ridden schools, and even in our teacher-training institutions? Perhaps rose-tinted human nature—pride, optimism, blindness, self-delusion, even self-interest—leads us to regard all our adversities as temporary blips on an untroubled horizon, to stay on the sinking ship. But problems can be insoluble, and when they are, it is better to recognize the fact. Disasters are a different state of affairs from problems, and call for a different kind of response. You have a problem when your roof leaks, and should try to find a way to patch it up. If the roof falls in on you, patching won't help. You have a disaster and should start tunneling your way out.

An Educational Disaster

I shall briefly examine "assessment" as an example of a current educational disaster. I could instead have selected accountability, ability-grouping, grading, curriculum design, special education, intervention programs, direct instruction, computer-based or computer-managed instruction, "excellence," "standards" (the latest smokescreen), educational bureaucracies, or a number of other manifestations of problem-solving fiddling while education burns. But assessment will do for now.

I recently attended a three-day conference of literacy teachers. The conference began and ended well with teachers talking about their classroom experiences and research. But the second day, entirely devoted to presentations and discussions on the topic of assessment, was a time-wasting shambles. People left more depressed and confused about assessment than when they arrived. The speakers clearly would have preferred to talk about their own teaching and their own students; but assessment had to be confronted, and they were doing the best they could. The audience wanted to hear of ways to do assessment that would interfere minimally with their normal lives, and would have preferred to hear that assessment was being abolished. No one believed that assessment would help beginners on their journey to literacy or teachers in their efforts to help readers, though a few well-intentioned people tried to find excuses for the pernicious practice. They couldn't believe that assessment had no redeeming features. But no one claimed that assessment solved a single problem.

I am not criticizing the organizers of the conference, in fact I think their planning made perfect sense. Assessment takes up at least a third of the time and energy of many classroom teachers, and the situation is getting worse, not better. As the "progress" that assessment is supposed to ensure fails to materialize, more and "better" assessment is expected to remedy the situation.

Assessment, or maintaining pressure on people caught in the system, is the only thing many politicians can think of when they take a problem-solving approach to education. George Bush claimed to be the Education President, but the best he could come up with for improving schools was to have more tests. In 1989, he called on state governors to find ways to make American education more effective. At that time, President Clinton was the chairperson of the National Governors' Association Education Panel. He called for tough national standards and for a national assessment system in core subjects. In Britain the government persistently takes the same approach. I am reminded of the old Mickey Rooney/Judy Garland movies on late-night television. Whenever the flagging plot begins to fall apart, Mickey suggests "Let's put on a show!" In education, the cry is always "Let's put on a test!"

Anyone would think that assessment was a new idea. But tests have been proliferating in education for the best part of a century, ever since their development within the eugenics movement. Since 1910 no fewer than 148 standardized reading and achievement tests for elementary students alone have been published in the United States—and only 34 of them have gone out of print (VanLeirsburg 1993). Presumably over a hundred are still in circulation and use, their numbers constantly increasing. Yet no one can demonstrate that any test has ever had a beneficial effect on education.

Even the people who want assessment are confused. I attended another conference that tried to dispose of the testing issue in the first hour. The district superintendent of instruction and assessment was supposed to outline his plans for new assessment procedures. He quickly revealed that he had no clear idea of what *he* expected to accomplish, let alone the teachers, and no idea of how assessment might help teachers, let alone students. All he wanted was *numbers*—of any kind—to pass on to other people. He could not relate teaching to testing except to admonish the teachers he was addressing not to teach to the tests, which added to their confusion. The conference barely recovered in the two days of serious work that followed the opening presentation.

Assessment has become a fully fledged disaster in its own right. It is discriminatory, and stigmatizes and disempowers individuals for life. It doesn't encourage anyone to read, write, learn, or think, though it does leave students and teachers frustrated, confused, despondent, resentful, and angry. I don't think assessment has any redeeming features, but if it has, an exorbitant price is paid for them. Assessment spawns difficulties faster than they can be dealt with. We don't need more tests, or better tests; we need to extricate ourselves from them.

The Growth of "Systems"

Charitably, I have been referring to education (and the economy) as a "system"—but this is a widespread misnomer. Systems, by definition, are organized, integrated, orderly, predictable, and functional. There is not a good term for what education is today—at least, not a euphemistic one. Education is disorganized and disorderly, unplanned and dysfunctional, a metastasizing growth, or an accident in progress.

We delude ourselves when we think of education (or the economy) as something coherent, logical, and rational that human beings have reflected upon, and *designed*, as a whole, with a clear purpose in mind, like the internal combustion engine, a jet airplane, or even the common kettle.

Chance has no doubt played its part in the development of automobile engines and other human artifacts, but by and large they have been designed and put together by people with a clear understanding of the place and purpose of each part and of the system as a whole. Parts that are unnecessary are discarded. Parts that don't do their job are replaced. Parts that work imperfectly are improved until superseded by a superior alternative. A visitor from outer space could inspect an automobile engine in working condition and figure out how and why it was conceived and constructed. I remember some good advice from the days when manuals for appliances made sense. Owners of a particular device were given a list of things that might go wrong, and for each fault briskly advised to "find problem and rectify." If the problem could not be promptly found and rectified, the device was to be replaced.

Education is not like that. Its various parts don't fit together as part of some coherently conceived whole. It is not a consequence of comprehensive planning or even of understanding. It has just grown. Since humans first walked the earth, people everywhere have doubtless tried to raise their young in their own idealized image, and tried also to help them to develop significant abilities. Different cultures cultivated different educational beliefs and customs, which weathered with time and changed as a result of contact, conflict, accident, and all manner of bright or crazy ideas. Education was never *planned*; it could always have been different.

There is no *ideal* education system. Education has always been too big to control, to comprehend, or even to *imagine* in all its detail. If education now appears impervious to change, it is not because it could not be any different—it clearly could and will be—but because of the vast inertial mass of its own complexity. Education doesn't advance; it drifts.

The uncontrolled and happenstantial development of education is not unique. This is the way most of the significant and universal influences in our lives have come about. Language is another example. Despite the widespread assumption, language is neither a rational design nor an ideal system. No one knows how language began—it is probably misleading even to think of language having a beginning. I suspect that it arose imperceptibly out of other aspects of people's lives, among different people, at different times and in different places, in different ways. No one designed or invented it. As people interacted across cultures and generations, language inevitably changed, but not in planned or predictable ways. All the languages of the world must be compatible with human physical and mental structures, but beyond those constraints they have always differed enormously, and still do today, with over three thousand languages and innumerable dialects still in existence.

Languages literally evolve. Every element of language has arisen by a kind of random mutation and survived by finding an ecological niche in the brains of human beings—by being useful and comprehensible, for a time at least. Sometimes people try a new way of saying something. Sometimes "mistakes" persist. Sometimes there is borrowing or adoption as languages come into contact. Some aspects of language grow, as people find new applications for them, while other aspects wither from disuse. No one is in control of the whole thing, or any significant part of it. Efforts to take charge of language inevitably fail. And efforts to change the way people use language are always limited and rarely lasting—language constantly gets away from us. It is like a turbulent stream that we can swim in but not divert.

Mathematics is the same. Mathematics doubtless developed in many small places in many small ways, just like language. No one planned where it should be today, and no one can foresee where it will be tomorrow. People wander through continents of mathematics that have been found and sometimes lost again in the past. More mathematics exists than any one person could know, and no group could claim to *direct* mathematics in any substantial way. It is what it is. It might easily have been different, and it will be different in the future.

Many other significant aspects of our lives have developed in the same uncontrollable way. The growth of cities has been largely unplanned and is beyond control despite all our efforts. Hydra-headed monsters cannot be controlled. The media are out of control. "News" is consumed faster than it is produced, the trivial is raised to ephemeral significance and the significant reduced to lasting triviality. Legal systems are out of control. More laws are written than anyone can read, let alone put into practice, and efforts to rationalize the "legal system" lead to even more laws, more confusions (and more lawyers). Publishing is out of control. Publishers can't afford to publish books that are different from those their competitors publish, and everyone concentrates on a few well-mined areas where a chance of substantial sales exists. The development and utilization of computer technology are clearly out of control; no one can keep up. I could go on, but I would get out of control myself.

One thing is always overlooked—*history*. Many people seem to think that history is something in the past that doesn't affect us now. But the reason we are where we are today with education, the economy, the internal combustion engine, language, mathematics, the law, and everything else, *is* history. We can't escape what has happened in the past; every incident has contributed to our present condition. History is not a series of steps by which we got to the present, it is the mold in which we are formed, the block of concrete in which our feet are inescapably set. History is not a problem we can "solve." Time can't be rolled back, and there are no orderly states to which situations that have become chaotic can be returned.

It may sound pessimistic and despairing to say that so much that seems central to our lives is beyond our control. But I don't feel that way. There are alternatives, if only we open our minds to them, and I maintain my faith in people (people in general, that is, not necessarily people in authority). We must simply stop trying to patch up the vessel we find ourselves on, lower the lifeboats, and row for new and probably unfamiliar shores. We have to begin by changing the way we think.

Changing the Way We Think
About Education

Many of our troubles in education arise from the fact that we are so concerned about *learning*. I would go so far as to suggest that all our talk about learning is counterproductive, and that we should (if we could control language) stop using the word. I know it will be argued that learning is the entire purpose of education, but that doesn't mean that it should demand all of our attention, or even most of it. Learning is an outcome, not a process, and if we focus only on the outcome, then we can easily get necessary preconditions all wrong.

Let me start with an analogy. We are concerned that children should grow physically, say an average of two inches a year over a particular period of their lives, and that their temperature should stay close to a healthy 98.6 degrees Fahrenheit. These are desirable outcomes, but in raising children we don't continually focus on the achievement of these states of affairs. We don't stretch or shrink children to ensure they are the right size, nor do we constantly warm or refrigerate them so that their temperature stays at the approved level. We are more concerned with clothing and nourishing them properly. Our concern is always (or should be) with those conditions in which growth is a natural and inevitable outcome.

Learning is simply an outcome, even a by-product. It is a consequence of experience (including imaginative experience) that is meaningful, that we can participate in and relate to ourselves. Since such experience involves personal identification and mutual collaboration, I refer to it metaphorically as "membership of clubs" (Smith 1988). We don't necessarily seek experience in order to learn (though learning may be part of the joy of many experiences)—our primary concern and aim is to have the experience, and learning follows. In education, we should ensure that students have access to appropriately "nourishing" experiences so that learning comes about naturally and inevitably.

Here's a foretaste of my final argument: we should concentrate our attention on the kinds of experience that students have in schools, not on what they learn. Learning comes with doing sensible and interesting things. We should not be concerned with *teaching* children to read (an outcome) but with *helping* them to read (a means, or series of experiences). Focussing on the reading outcome leads to bizarre behavior and attitudes, from the mindless promotion of "skill-based" exercises to diagnoses of imaginary mental deficiencies. Focussing on experience means that every child has optimum opportunity for the outcome to occur naturally. As many researchers have shown, and Krashen (1993) has very conveniently summarized, "free voluntary reading" results in students learning just about everything that we strive so hard to teach them about reading, and much more besides.

Learning is usually seen as an incremental activity. We are supposed to learn by adding bits of knowledge or information to the store we have already accumulated. Every new thing learned is another block added to the tower of what we know already, another item in the cognitive data-bank. Occasionally we talk about learning as "growth" or "development," but we are usually not referring to the way a tree or the human body grows. Natural growth is not additive. Babies don't grow by having successive inches added to their height. The increase in their height is simply an indicator that the entire organism has developed, not necessarily at the same rate or in the same proportion in all directions. A twenty-pound baby is not 2 ten-pound babies, one on top of the other, nor does the larger infant have more limbs or more organs.

Learning, like physical growth, is not a consequence of external pressure; we don't even learn as a result of trying harder. All of us have experienced failure to learn something we wanted to learn, despite intense motivation and effort. Yet other things we make no particular effort to memorize—like major news items, gossip, the scores in a sport in which we are interested, and even the antics of characters in television sitcoms—seem to become imprinted on our mind without effort.

The reason is the difference between learning and rote memorization, which boosters of testing and instructional planning totally overlook. Deliberate memorization, such as rehearsing facts until we take a test, or holding a telephone number in mind until we can dial it, requires effort. The forced ingestion of facts and data is useless for educational purposes. It has a half-life of a few hours. We rarely remember after the examination anything we tried to cram into our minds before it. What we remember from fruitless efforts to memorize are the stress and the failure inevitably involved.

Learning is like physical growth; it usually occurs without our being aware of it; it is long-lasting, and requires a nurturing environment. It takes place as a result of social relationships (including relationships with authors of books or with characters in books) and pivots on personal identification. We learn from the kind of person we see ourselves as being like, or expect to be like. Such conditions are annihilated by information-transmission teaching and constant tests.

Saving Ourselves and Our Students

I have a couple of suggestions about how teachers might begin to save themselves and their students from the over-controlled, over-managed, over-systematized, and over-researched disaster that is education. The first is to change the way we talk about schools, and the second is to change the way we behave in them.

We should change the way we talk about schools by talking less about learning and teaching, and more about *doing*. When we focus on teaching specific skills, students frequently fail to learn them and rarely become enthusiastic about engaging in them voluntarily. When we concern ourselves with engaging students in interesting and comprehensible activities, then they learn. They may not all learn at the same time, at the same rate, and even with the same enthusiasm, but individual variation is inevitable; it has to be recognized and accepted. Homogenization never works in education, nor should we want or expect it to.

Doesn't this conflict with my remarks about being unable to control language? Quite the reverse; we must accept that the meaning of the words *teach* and *learn* has changed, and therefore try to modify the way in which we use them. "Teach" once meant "show" and "learn" meant "to hear about something," but now the words are more likely to be defined as the "dissemination" (or transmission) and "acquisition" of information and knowledge. We may not be able to change other people's use of the words, but we can focus attention on what actually is going on in the name of teaching and learning in schools.

Instead of talking all the time about what teachers should teach and what students should learn, we should talk about what teachers and students should *do*. We should talk about experiences that they should be mutually engaged in, involving reading, writing, imagining, creating, calculating, constructing, producing, and performing. You can't think of any? Sorry, but you must use your imagination (and that of your students), not rely on experts or authorities outside the classroom to tell you.

I am talking about the *climate* of classrooms and schools. Like the climate of the world outside, the climate of a classroom is very easy to detect. You don't have to ask anyone if it is raining as you walk down a street, nor do you need any special tests to find out if the sun is shining. You just have to look to see if the streets are wet or sunny.

You don't need to ask anyone or to apply formal tests to see if everyone in a classroom is engaged in meaningful activity—you just look. It is easy to see if the students—and the teacher—are interested, engaged, and collaborative or bored, confused, and withdrawn. (Of course, students have to be present, and behaving normally. There's not much to learn if the classroom is empty, or if all the students stand respectfully mute and immobile in the visitor's presence.)

We must get away from the idea that everything would be fine with our educational institutions if only teachers and students worked harder. That is why we should no longer talk about schools in the language that has made them what they are today. Attempting to "improve" or expand the current ritual of schools will only make them worse. Education is on the wrong track, largely because of "solutions" which have socially isolated teachers and students from each other and from sensible ways of spending their time.

Lifeboats

"Save women and children first" is supposed to be the call when a ship is going down. Only slightly amended to "Save teachers and students first," it might also be considered an appropriate cry for education. Don't cling to the doomed structure of the foundering educational system, but strike out to save the passengers and crew. (Officers on the bridge, of course, would prefer to go down with the ship.)

How should teachers save themselves and their students? By getting themselves into lifeboats which can survive the turbulent waters and making their way to secure havens. What are these lifeboats? Any situation that preserves the self-respect of teachers and students, the kinds of situation I have already referred to that naturally involve reading, writing, and other things that we want students to learn. These are the activities we should concentrate upon in classrooms, free of pressure or manipulation from outside.

Added to this should be some consciousness raising so that teachers and students come to a better realization of the educational leviathan into whose service they have been press-ganged, and the directions in which it is currently being navigated. It is unfortunate when teachers believe that the system they work in is rational and functional—so that any failure must be their own—and a tragedy when students learn to believe the same thing.

All teachers do good things some of the time and all good teachers do bad things some of the time. Differences among teachers lie not only in the proportions of the good and the bad, but also in their awareness of the effects of what they are doing and in their readiness to share this awareness with their students. While striving always to do more of the beneficial and less of the damaging, teachers must also protect themselves and their students from adverse aspects of their situation that can't immediately be changed.

I can hear a lot of people on the rails of the *Titanic* looking down at the lifeboats bobbing on the cold ocean, and objecting, "Yes, but. . . ."

Yes, but—we live in a culture based on grades. Parents want grades, students want grades, and parents want to know how well their children are doing relative to other students in the class. Such demands only demonstrate the extent of the disaster. Parents and students have been "educated" to believe that what the system has become is more important than what the system is supposed to do. At one time it would have been ludicrous for parents interested in knowing what their children were learning at school to be fobbed off with a grade point average or a relative position in the class. They would want to know what their children could *do*.

Yes, but—you're not giving us any *specific* suggestions about what teachers should do when they cast off from the ship. That's because I don't have any specific suggestions, and because I don't believe that anyone has the right to tell teachers what to do, or any teacher the right to expect to be told. Decisions should be made in the lifeboats, not on the sinking liner or from the distant shore. Teachers should *know* when their students are doing (and learning) worthwhile things, and when their students are doing (and learning) things that will be damaging to their personal and social development. (If teachers don't know that, they shouldn't be in a classroom.) Teachers need support, and they need to share experience, but the way to achieve these ends is among their peers, through collegiality, not through hierarchical structures. Teachers must save themselves, and they can best do that by observing and supporting each other.

The educational system may not be amenable to change, but people are. Every school situation that is interesting, comprehensible, and encouraging for the teachers and students concerned is another lifeboat launched, another chance to survive disaster. This is something all teachers should understand—and encouragingly there are many who already do so. And if teachers can't get their students into one lifeboat, they must ensure they get aboard another. There must be enough lifeboats to shuttle teachers and students from the disaster of the educational system to islands where they can, with mutual respect, engage in sensible and stimulating activities, the sole justification for education.

Perkins, David. 1981. *The Mind's Best Work*. Cambridge, MA: Harvard University Press.

Rosen, Harold. 1986. "The Importance of Story." *Language Arts*, 63(3), 226–37.

———. 1988. "Stories of Stories: Footnotes on Sly Gossipy Practices." In *The Word for Teaching is Learning: Essays for James Britton*, edited by Martin Lightfoot and Nancy Martin. London: Heinemann Educational Books.

Rosenblatt, Louise M. 1978. *The Reader: The Text: The Poem*. Carbondale, IL: Southern Illinois University Press.

———. 1980. "What Facts Does This Poem Teach You?" *Language Arts*, 57(4), 386–94.

Rosset, Clement. 1989. "Reality and the Untheorizable." In *The Limits of Theory*, edited by Thomas M. Kavanagh. Stanford, CA: Stanford University Press.

Sacks, Oliver. 1989. *Seeing Voices: A Journey into the World of the Deaf*. Berkeley, CA: University of California Press.

Scollon, Suzanne B. K., and Ron Scollon. 1981. *Narrative, Literacy, and Face in Interethnic Communication*. Norwood, NJ: Ablex Publishing.

Scribner, Sylvia, and Michael Cole. 1978. "Literacy Without Schooling: Testing for Intellectual Effects." *Harvard Educational Review*, 48(4), 448–61.

Shannon, Patrick. 1985. "Reading Instruction and Social Class." *Language Arts*, 62(6), 604–13.

Smith, Frank. 1983. *Essays into Literacy*. Portsmouth, NH: Heinemann Educational Books.

———. 1985. *Reading Without Nonsense*. 2d ed. New York: Teachers College Press.

———. 1986. *Insult to Intelligence*. Portsmouth, NH: Heinemann Educational Books.

———. 1988. *Joining the Literacy Club*. Portsmouth, NH: Heinemann Educational Books.

———. 1990. *to think*. New York: Teachers College Press.

———. 1993. *Whose Language? What Power?* New York: Teachers College Press.

———. 1994. *Understanding Reading*. 5th ed. Hillside, NJ: Lawrence Erlbaum Associates.

VanLeirsburg, Peggy. 1993. "Standardized Reading Tests: Then and Now." In *Literacy: Celebration and Challenge*, edited by Jerry L. Johns. Bloomington, IL: Illinois Reading Council.

Vincente, Kim J., and William F. Brewer. 1993. "Reconstructive Remembering of the Scientific Literature." *Cognition*, 46, 101–28.

Weaver, Constance. 1988. *Reading Process and Practice*. Portsmouth, NH: Heinemann Educational Books.

Willinski, John. 1990. *The New Literacy: Redefining Reading and Writing in the Schools*. London: Routledge.

Name Index

Anderson, Richard C., 25, 99

Barr, Rebecca, 59
Brewer, William J., 100
Bruner, Jerome S., 8, 19
Bush, George, 107

Campbell, Donald T., 100
Clinton, Bill, 107
Cole, Michael, 54
Conrad, Joseph, 13
Cronbach, Lee J., 101
Csikszentmihalyi, Mihalyi, 3

Eliot, T.S., 8

Farnan, Nancy, 98
Fiske, Donald W., 100
Flood, James, 98
Freire, Paulo, 61

Garland, Judy, 107
Giroux, Henry A., 56
Goelman, Hillel, 44

Herman, Patricia A., 25
Hillocks, George, 98

James, William, 8

Krashen, Stephen D., 23, 24, 25, 111

Lapp, Diane, 98
Luria, Aleksandr R., 6

Meek, Margaret, 25, 45, 61
Melville, Herman, 13
Mikulecky, Larry, 55

Nagy, William E., 25

Oberg, Antoinette A., 44
Olson, David R., 23, 54

Perkins, David, 9
Pound, Ezra, 8

Rooney, Mickey, 107
Rosen, Harold, 8, 19
Rosset, Clement, 35

Subject Index

age and ability grouping, 82
assessment, 106–108; *see also* evaluation
authors, 45

brain, 1–14, 37; business of, 12–13

change in education, 51–52, 111–115; *see also* schools, change
classroom, climate of, 113; ideal, 86
clubs, 20–21, joining, 41; spoken language club, 18–19
cognitive science, 83
communication, 15–16, 38
comprehension, 2–3, 35–36
computers, *see* technology, electronic; information highway

decoding, 28
definitions, 34–37
demonstrations, 12–13
disasters, 105–106, educational, 106–108
discrimination, 22, 25–26, 82

education, language of, 26; as a system, 108–109
evaluation, 58–59, 82, 91, 106–108
experience, 29–34
eye movements, 28

failure in school, 81
forgetting, 43

grades, 86, 114–115, *see also* evaluation
growth, 112

hyperbole, 57

identity, 17–26, 80–82
imagination, 7–9
information, 15–17
information highway, 69–72, 73–77
insight, 9–10
instruction, overselling, 56–57
integration, 88–89
interest, 33–34
intuition, 9–10